the LEAGUE of PARDONED REBELS

ENDORSEMENTS

"Derrick's passion for teaching and applying Scripture is present in his examination of each disciple. Both laity and clergy will be challenged and encouraged when reading this book."

—Dr. Jeff Audirsch,
Professor of Old Testament and Hebrew, New Orleans Baptist Theological Seminary, New Orleans, LA

"Derrick's book, masterfully titled, is more timely today than ever before. Given the Church's wholesale abandonment of discipleship and decreasing appetite for following the life-giving way of our Messiah, Derrick's voice is a refreshing call to reclaim what's been lost and give our lives fully to Him."

—Rev. Biz Gainey,
Senior Pastor, Pillar Community Church, Vero Beach, FL

"I would use this book as a source for preaching on the disciples."

—Dr. Benjie Loyd,
Senior Pastor, River Road Baptist Church, Hillard, FL

"Derrick is an excellent thinker, who has put truth over tribe. He serves the Church well."

—Dr. Jay Sanders,
Chair of Biblical Studies, Strong Rock Christian School, Locust Grove, GA

"Derrick has a gift for explaining the Bible, and he challenges the wise with his depth of insight in this book."

—Rev. Greg Sempsrott,
Senior Pastor, Vero Bible Fellowship, Vero Beach, FL

the LEAGUE of PARDONED REBELS

DERRICK WEST

with foreword by DR. CRAIG CULBRETH
and REV. TIM O'CARROLL

Ambassador International
Greenville, South Carolina & Belfast, Northern Ireland
www.ambassador-international.com

The League of Pardoned Rebels
©2020 by Derrick West
All rights reserved

ISBN: 978-1-64960-015-8
eISBN: 978-1-64960-016-5

Cover Design and Typesetting by Hannah Nichols
eBook edition by Anna Riebe Raats

All rights reserved. No part of this book may be used or reproduced in any manner whatsoever without written permission except in the case of brief quotations embodied in critical articles or reviews.

The Greek New Testament. Stuttgart, Germany: Deutsche Bibelgesellschaft, 1998.

The Holy Bible, King James Version. New York, NY: American Bible Society, 1999.

New International Version. Nashville, TN: Zondervan, 2011.

The New American Standard Bible. Anaheim, CA: Lockman Foundation Publications, 1995.

The New King James Version. Nashville, TN: Thomas Nelson, 1982.

AMBASSADOR INTERNATIONAL
Emerald House
411 University Ridge, Suite B14
Greenville, SC 29601, USA
www.ambassador-international.com

AMBASSADOR BOOKS
The Mount
2 Woodstock Link
Belfast, BT6 8DD, Northern Ireland, UK
www.ambassadormedia.co.uk

The colophon is a trademark of Ambassador, a Christian publishing company.

I dedicate *The League of Pardoned Rebels* to the following:

Jeff Audirsch

Craig Culbreth

Biz Gainey

Steve Laufer

Benjie Loyd

Rob Moore

Marc McCain

Tim O'Carroll

Josh Palmer

Matt Parris

Jay Sanders

Greg Sempsrott

My friends, if not for the grace of our Lord Jesus, we would still be unpardoned rebels, dead in our transgressions and sins.

"Come lose your life for a carpenter's son
For a madman who died for a dream
And you'll have the faith his first followers had
And you'll feel the weight of the beam."

— Michael Card, *God's Own Fool*

CONTENTS

FOREWORD — 11

INTRODUCTION
AN INSIDE INVITATION — 13

CHAPTER 1
THE MOUNTAINS OF GOD — 17

CHAPTER 2
AND JESUS CALLED HIM SIMON PETER — 27

CHAPTER 3
JAMES, SON OF ZEBEDEE, AND
THE GOSPEL EXCHANGE — 41

CHAPTER 4
JOHN, THE DISCIPLE JESUS LOVED — 53

CHAPTER 5
THE ANDREW CALLING — 67

CHAPTER 6
FINDING PHILIP — 77

CHAPTER 7
NATHANAEL: WITHOUT GUILE, BUT
FULL OF PREJUDICE — 87

CHAPTER 8
MATTHEW: THE VILEST OFFENDER
WHO TRULY BELIEVED — 97

CHAPTER 9
THOMAS: THE FIRST DOUBTER
AMONG EQUALS — 109

CHAPTER 10
THE ZEALOT'S CROSS   119

CHAPTER 11
JAMES, THE SON OF ALPHAEUS   129

CHAPTER 12
THE JUDAS ISCARIOT DISGUISE   137

CHAPTER 13
JUDAS, NOT ISCARIOT: THE
DISCIPLE WITH ONE LINE   147

CONCLUSION
SIX HONEST-SERVING MEN: WHAT,
WHY, WHEN, HOW, WHERE, AND WHO   155

CHALLENGE: SO, THEREFORE,
BASIN AND TOWEL DISCIPLESHIP   169

FOR FURTHER READING   175

BIBLIOGRAPHY   177

DISCOGRAPHY   189

ENDNOTES   193

ACKNOWLEDGMENTS

Thank you, Dawn, Miller, and Sam for your unconditional love.

Thank you, Mom and Dad, for breaking my Nintendo, so I would read.

Thank you, Genesis Church of Vero Beach, for believing in me and loving me in spite of what you know about me.

Thank you, Jon Hamilton and Rachel Walker, for reading this manuscript and encouraging me to publish it.

Thank you, Anna Raats and your fine team of professionals at Ambassador International.

Thank you, Katie Cruice Smith and your intern for the summer of 2019. Both of your editing prowess, professionalism, and constructive criticism tops my chalkboard eraser-throwing English Literature teacher in high school.

Most of all, thank You, Jesus. I still stand amazed in Your presence because I am but a worm apart from Your mercy.

FOREWORD

MANY EXCELLENT BOOKS HAVE MORE stellar forewords. We are not seeking to write a brilliant foreword; we pen it instead to share some thoughts with you as you begin the journey of reading *The League of Pardoned Rebels*. The book is an incredible read and a fantastic resource. We love the edge of it, and Derrick's observations throughout the pages challenge us to think through each disciple's life in great detail.

In this book, we come to understand that the original twelve disciples, whom we so often look up to and want to model our lives after, were just ordinary men. They missed the mark over and over, but each time, the grace of God covered them.

He equally reminds all of us that Bible characters didn't know they played a role in God's Book. They never got out of bed, thinking, *I am a Bible character; how should I therefore act?* Derrick observes the good and bad in each of them; just as they appear in the Bible.

The *League of Pardoned Rebels* also helps us to see that we don't know how our story ends. Only God finishes our script. We have to walk by faith, just as the disciples did.

We believe Derrick is a man of God who seeks to touch and change the world with his preaching, teaching, and leadership in the local church and in how he lives out his daily life. We also know how committed he is to the Word of God and how it plays out in the culture of today.

I, Tim, have had the privilege of walking with Derrick throughout Israel. We walked around the Sea of Galilee and through the streets of Jerusalem, where the disciples walked with Jesus. He has a tremendous wealth of wisdom that you will notice within the pages of this book.

He connects the Old Testament with the New Testament in a creative way through the lives of the disciples. Further, he reminds us that the same Jesus Whom each of the disciples had to follow was sufficient enough for all of them. They equally had the same needs: a sacrifice for sins and resurrection power.

Take your time reading the book and be sure to meditate on the questions Derrick asks at the end of each chapter. His ability to express himself in the way he does in the book will help you see your value through the lives of the disciples. They swam upstream in their down-stream world—just as Derrick does, and just as God calls you to do.

We all must come to a place of holy surrender to the Lordship of Jesus Christ, regardless of our knowledge of Him. After all, we who claim to be followers of Jesus are a part of the same League of Pardoned Rebels. May we never take this for granted and live a life of purpose as we walk in the grace of our Savior.

Dr. Craig Culbreth,
Regional Catalyst East, The Florida Baptist Convention
and
Rev. Tim O'Carroll,
Director of the Treasure Coast Baptist Association

Introduction

AN INSIDE INVITATION

THIRTY YEARS AGO, MY MOM and dad took me to a Ringling Bros. and Barnum & Bailey Circus. I remember the parade outside the circus tent like it happened yesterday. There were "lions and tigers and bears, oh my"[1] en route to make their grand entrance inside the tent. I had a particular affinity for Dumbo Junior, all dressed to the nines in his finely tailored garb befitting of an elephant about to perform a balancing routine that would have landed me a first-class ambulance ride to the hospital.

What surprised me, though, was the difference between those who gathered to watch the parade from those who went inside the tent to see the show. The massive parade crowd dispersed rather quickly after all of the pomp and circumstance. Just those who wanted to see the show and had a ticket went inside.

The call to follow Jesus is an invitation to do just that: follow Him inside the tent. Christ the Lord did not come into this world to make interested observers. He came to make disciples who listen to His Spirit and live by and in His truth, right there inside the tent of His abiding presence.

The word *disciple* comes from the Greek word *mathetes,* meaning "pupil, or follower."[2] Jesus used it to describe what he desired from the Twelve and from you and me. He wants to teach us about His character through fellowship with Him so that we can be ambassadors of His Kingdom. If we don't, we'll fashion Jesus from figments of our imagination and lead people astray. But if we do, we'll change the world, one heart at a time.

I am not very good at creating disciples in my image. I get frustrated when they turn out to be different from me. Thankfully, Jesus is the opposite of me. He penned His hope for all of humanity on a cast of characters more suited for a second-rate television talk show episode than those divinely entrusted to announce the way God was going to relate to humanity from that point forward.

From "the vilest tax offender who truly believed"[3] like Matthew to a terrorist named Simon the Zealot, Jesus put these twelve individuals together for a reason. Though they came from different backgrounds and had varying views of the world, Jesus made them teammates so they all would see their equality at the foot of Calvary first. Then they joined hand in hand and glorified Him collectively by showing those they encountered that their Savior *is* merciful, forgiving, infinitely kind, and graceful through the way they loved and related to each other.

According to Jesus, "The student is not above the teacher, nor a servant above his master" (Matt. 10:24).

The League of Pardoned Rebels learned this axiom from experience. Some were malleable. Jesus had to soften others through the Refiner's fire. All but one came to Him the same way we do: by grace through faith alone.

Jesus didn't become flesh and dwell among us (John 1:14) to make us church members content with following Him from a distance. He came to make disciples willing to think as He thought, teach as He taught, love as He loved, sacrifice as He sacrificed, and serve as He served. Because He knew if He created a metamorphosis in the hearts of a few, they would change the world; and they did.[4]

His league is open now, but the application process starts inside the tent. The entry fee will cost you nothing because it was paid for you two thousand years ago in Jerusalem on a cruel Roman cross. The monthly dues, however, are quite costly but well worth the price.

Want to change the world? Come inside the tent and continue reading. If not, give your book to someone who does.

They were the League of Pardoned Rebels. What follows is their God's story, and it's your story, too. Be sure to read each chapter through the lens of prayer, and I've included some reflection questions at the end of each chapter to make your study more personal. As their journey becomes yours, my prayer is that the Holy Spirit, Who enlightened and mobilized the Twelve to be the hands and feet of Christ in their world, will do the same for you in yours.

SOME QUESTIONS TO PONDER BEFORE MOVING ON

1. What does the title of the book suggest about how God relates to His people?

2. Read James 2:19. How does a belief in Jesus that is demonstrated by obedience to Him differ from the type of belief that James describes?

3. Read Matthew 11:28-30. In what areas of your life do you need assurance that His "yoke is easy" and His "burden is light"? Commit them to Him right now.

Chapter 1

THE MOUNTAINS OF GOD

I ONCE CLIMBED A MOUNTAIN in Israel called Masada. It was enough for me not to invest in an Everest expedition anytime soon. The arduous journey up the slope demanded I rest at her summit. Firmly perched on a boulder at the top, all I did was breathe heavily and enjoy the view. I looked in one direction and saw the Dead Sea. Gazing in another direction allowed my eyes to focus in on a resplendent garden in the middle of all the aridness some distance away. My response to the beauty before me was a prayer of thanksgiving to the Lord for what He spoke into existence *ex nihilo*, "out of nothing."[5]

MOUNTAINS AS SPIRITUAL EXPERIENCES

On many occasions in the Scriptures, writers used mountains as figures of speech to denote God's character. "As the mountains surround Jerusalem, so the Lord surrounds his people both now and forevermore," wrote the psalmist about His protection in Psalm 125:2. Mount Sinai "quaked before the Lord" when God gave His moral decrees to Moses (Judg. 5:5).

On other occasions, they denote a spiritual climb or ascent. In the mind of the ancients, God's abode was in Heaven, so climbing a mountain was equivalent to drawing closer to God Himself. That's one reason why the great heroes of the Scriptures—including Jesus—did it. It's also why the psalmist lifts his "eyes to the mountains" to look for help from the "Maker of heaven and earth" (Psalm 121:1-2).

When we fellowship with Jesus, we ascend the mountain by pursuing him the way David did. He was *after* God in his life (1 Sam. 13:14) because he wanted to know His character. During his pursuit, David found out that catching Him required clean hands and a heart free from idolatry and falsehood (Psalm 24:3-4). Elijah climbed Mount Carmel and called down fire from Heaven on the false prophets of Baal for the same reason (1 Kings 18:16-39). As a result, God rewarded their climbs.

MOUNTAINS AS COVENANT LOCATIONS

Search the Scriptures, and you will find that mountains are also scenes for *every* significant covenant where God legislated His terms for His people. The word *covenant* appears eighty-eight times in the first five books of the Bible alone. It's an essential word that should govern our thinking about how the materials from Genesis to Revelation relate to each other.

We often confuse a covenant with a contract. If I sign a legal contract with a potential buyer of my lawn dart collection and he doesn't keep his end of the bargain by paying me, the deal is null and void. On the other hand, a covenant denotes relationships. It's an agreement two parties make with the understanding that if one party doesn't keep the terms of it, the connection remains, albeit fractured.

In biblical covenants, God never fails to keep His covenantal terms. I do quite frequently, though. And when I fail miserably, He draws me back to Himself—by whatever means necessary—because He loves me. That's what being in a covenant relationship with Him is all about. It's the basis for how He relates to us and we to Him.

ARARAT AND NOAH

God baptized Noah into a covenant relationship with Him on Ararat, where the ark just happened to rest after the flood. God blessed him there, saying:

"This is the sign of the covenant I am making between me and you and every living creature with you, a covenant for all generations to come: I have set my rainbow in the clouds, and it will be the sign of the covenant between me and the earth. Whenever I bring clouds over the earth and the rainbow appears in the clouds, I will remember my covenant between me and you and all living creatures of every kind. Never again will the waters become a flood to destroy all life. Whenever the rainbow appears in the clouds, I will see it and remember the everlasting covenant between God and all the living creatures of every kind on the earth" (Gen. 9:12-16).

Before the Flood, creation spiraled downward because of wickedness. Noah, however, "found favor in the eyes of the Lord" (Gen. 6:8) when he believed by faith a flood was coming and obeyed God's command to build an ark (Gen. 6:22, 7:5). The covenant the Lord made with Noah applied to all of creation, implying life itself is valuable to God. And Noah's faith and obedience rewarded on Mount Ararat is the key to understanding what Jesus looks for in every person who walks the face of the Earth.

MOREH, MORIAH, AND ABRAHAM

As Ararat was to Noah, Moreh and Moriah were to Abraham. Without them, Father Abraham doesn't have many sons.[6] Without them, I'm not one of them, and neither are you. Without them, we can't just praise the Lord. But because of them, we can.

At Moreh, God reaffirmed His promises of land and descendants to Abraham (Gen. 12:7). Though he responded with enormous faith (Gen. 12:8), Abraham pawned his wife off to the pharaoh of Egypt during a famine in the next scene because he doubted God (Gen. 12:10-13).

When Isaac, the child of the promise, arrived via Sarah, God tested Abraham at Moriah. The Almighty designed it precisely because of the famous patriarch's proclivity for doubting Him. What a test it was, too! "Then

God said, 'Take your son, your only son, whom you love—Isaac—and go to the region of Moriah. Sacrifice him there as a burnt offering on a mountain I will show you'" (Gen. 22:2). I would have failed that one.

But before you label the Lord as cruel here, remember the reason for the test. Will God change His mind on a whim about the child of the promise? That was Abraham's quandary. Which Abraham will show up—the doubter or the believer? That was his test.

Fortunately, we know the answer to those questions. The angel of the Lord stopped him from doing what he didn't want to do and provided a suitable substitute (Gen. 22:11-13). Then, God asserted Himself:

> "I swear by myself, declares the Lord, that <u>because</u> you have done this and have not withheld your son, your only son, I will surely bless you and make your descendants as numerous as the stars in the sky and as the sand on the seashore. Your descendants will take possession of the cities of their enemies, and through your offspring all nations on earth will be blessed, because you have obeyed me" (Gen. 22:16-18—emphasis mine).

Look closely at the underlined word above. Now, look at the promises that follow it. It's the first time faith became the reason for the Lord's blessings. While Noah's faith and obedience led to the grace of life itself, Abraham's faith became the basis for God establishing His covenant people, a lesson he learned at the Divine laboratories of Moreh and Moriah.

HOREB, PISGAH, SINAI, AND MOSES

Moses climbed Sinai and received the Ten Commandments via the finger of God (Exod. 31:18). It wasn't the only mountain he climbed either. He was quite the summit addict!

On Horeb, Moses encountered the burning bush and received instructions to remove his sandals because of the sacredness of God's presence there (Exod. 3:1, 5). He also obeyed the Lord's instructions to strike a rock on Horeb so that water could flow for the Israelites to drink (Exod. 17:6).

Unfortunately, though, Moses disobeyed the next time the Lord wanted to hydrate the Israelites courtesy of a rock (Num. 20:11). Because he did, the Lord put a moratorium on his entry into the Promised Land (Num. 20:12), just like I had to do with my kids eating at McDonald's when they decided to see if French fries could fly to other tables. Moses could only view the land from the top of Pisgah, where he died (Deut. 34:1-7).

At Sinai, the most famous mountain in the Bible, God cut his covenant with Moses. This alp is the scene for Exodus chapters twenty through forty, the whole book of Leviticus, and Numbers one through eight. The themes of salvation, righteousness, and worship—in that order—govern the narrative.

God saved the Israelites by bringing them out of Egypt (Exod. 20:1-2). Then He gave them His commands because He wanted His covenant people to live righteously (Exod. 20:3-17, 21:1-24:18). He followed that with instructions on how to build the tabernacle and make sacrifices there (Exod. 25-Lev. 27).

The Lord of covenants dictated the terms of His relationship to Moses in that sequence for a reason. Without salvation, righteousness is hollow, and worship doesn't make sense. Salvation without regard for walking in righteousness leads to a guilt-ridden conscience and a lack of joy in the worship experience. Israel had to learn that before they left the base of Sinai en route to the Promised Land.

Unfortunately, though, even Moses, the most significant hero of the Old Testament, wasn't exempt from God's standards. Because the Almighty takes sin and disobedience personally, Moses couldn't enter Canaan.

If Horeb and Pisgah could speak, they would agree. They would also tell us that a prophet like Moses (Deut. 18:15) has come. When He did, He instituted a New Covenant and announced it on mountains with sermons (Matt. 5-7), transfigurations (Matt. 17:1-9), and discourses about the future (Matt. 24-25) so that we could become the righteousness of God in Him (2 Cor. 5:21). And they would tell us unapologetically that the Prophet's name is Jesus.

THE MOUNT OF OLIVES, MORIAH, ZION, AND DAVID

The Lord's covenant with King David was unconditional. After David had Bathsheba's husband killed for illicit purposes and repented of his sin(Psalm 51), Nathan prophesied: "When your days are over and you go to be with your ancestors, I will raise up your offspring to succeed you, one of your own sons, and I will establish his kingdom. He is the one who will build a house for me, and I will <u>establish his throne forever</u>" (1 Chron. 17:11-12—emphasis mine).

The word forever means just that: forever. David was hardly the bastion of family values after repenting of his sins. He fled to the Mount of Olives because his son, Absalom, wanted him dead (2 Sam. 15:30). His other son, Solomon, built high places to pagan gods there to appease his wives (1 Kings 11:7-8). This covenant was not about David, Solomon, or Absalom, though. It was about God's purpose in the world, regardless of whether they said amen or acted becomingly.

For this reason, God moved David to buy the threshing floor of Araunah the Jebusite on Moriah—the same place of Abraham's faith experience (2 Sam. 24:18-25). Sometime later, Solomon built the temple there (2 Chron. 3:1). What was a mountain of Divine revelation for Abraham became the location of fellowship for God's covenant people. The temple's beauty even inspired the Sons of Korah to label it Zion (Psalm 48:2, 11-12).

Unfortunately, that Zion can't speak to us today because it was reduced to rubble by the Babylonians in 586 BCE. But the Cornerstone of the New Zion (1 Peter 2:6), Christ the Lord, can enunciate quite clearly because His Zion, the city of the living God, is a fortress in the hearts of His covenant people.

SO, THEREFORE, JESUS CLIMBED A MOUNTAIN

When you see the word *therefore* in the Bible, you should always ask what it is "there for." The same is true for the one above. Noah heard from God on a mountain; Abraham, Moses, David, and Jesus did, too. Mark tells us what happened after our Lord's conversation with His Father: "These are the twelve he appointed: Simon (to whom he gave the name Peter), James son of Zebedee and his brother John (to them he gave the name Boanerges, which means sons of thunder), Andrew, Philip, Bartholomew, Matthew, Thomas, James son of Alphaeus, Thaddaeus, Simon the Zealot and Judas Iscariot, who betrayed him" (Mark 3:16-19).

If I knew I was going to be responsible for handpicking individuals to usher in the New Covenant, I would sign up movers and shakers with last names like Rockefeller, Roosevelt, Vanderbilt, and Carnegie. Jesus didn't. Notice those brothers nicknamed Boanerges? They had severe anger management issues. I assuredly would have scratched them from my list. Jesus, however, sought and then mobilized them.

See that man nicknamed Zealot? That means he was a terrorist. He would have thought nothing of killing Matthew, who was a tax collector before he met Jesus. I would have taken a pass on both and called the law on one of them. But Jesus didn't. He handpicked them to usher in the New Covenant.

It was a covenant that turned cowards into uncompromising leaders and made angry brothers benevolent ones. It forced tax collectors and terrorists to see each other through charitable eyes. It was a plan that would not fail, even though one very well-spoken, winsome, wealthy, deeply religious, and well-connected fellow among them tried to wreck it because he chose greed and deceit as virtues, consequently fellowshipping with the devil when Jesus needed him the most. God, after all, had spoken to His Son on a mountain and commissioned Him to institute a New World Order, and it would come to pass.

Yes, you read that right. I said New World Order. It's not a misprint or bad phrase choice. The number twelve symbolizes Divine government in the Scriptures. There were twelve tribes of Israel (Deut. 33:6-25) and twelve judges in the Book of Judges. Aaron's high priestly breastplate had twelve ephods, one for every tribe (Exod. 28:21). Solomon appointed twelve officers to his royal court (1 Kings 4:7). According to John's Revelation, a sign from heaven featuring a "woman clothed with the sun, with the moon under her feet" wore a crown containing twelve stars (Rev. 12:1); and the New Jerusalem brought to Earth by God Himself features twelve pearly gates, each one manned by an angel (Rev. 21:12).

Jesus taught His disciples to pray these words: "Your kingdom come, your will be done on earth as it is in heaven" (Matt. 6:10). His greatest desire for them was for His divine government, which originates from His eternal throne in Heaven, to be brought about on Earth. And He entrusted them, the Twelve, to institute it.

SO WHAT

We are broken people, unable even in our best effort to keep the standards of God. As a result, we are in desperate need of sustaining love, grace, truth, and mercy, even if we don't want to admit it. Knowing this, Jesus called to Himself twelve individuals who knew they couldn't keep His righteous standards because rebelling against what God had spoken was as instinctive to them as breathing.

Instead of receiving condemnation, which they all deserved, Jesus pardoned them and then entrusted them to model a new way of relating to God through the eyes of unconditional love and mercy. Such Divine wisdom was our Lord's great political statement relative to the issues of His day. That's His politick to us now.

Jesus learned that on the mountain of God—as did His disciples and the Galileans listening to Him preach a famous sermon on one. We will, too, if we take the time to climb up the mountain because inside this tent of discipleship, God has a peak there for each of us to ascend. It's one where He teaches us by His Spirit and from His Word. You don't have to summit before fellowshipping and resting in His presence there either. He's present now and willing to walk with you every step of the way.

Here is the thing, though: you have to be willing to go inside the tent first. "If none go with me, still I will follow,"[7] as the old song says. What about you?

SOME QUESTIONS TO PONDER BEFORE MOVING ON

1. How much noise fills your day? How much of it includes contemplative silence?

2. Read Exodus 19:1-6 and Mark 3:13-21. Why do you think Jesus and Moses heard the voice of God on a mountain?

3. In what ways can you incorporate more contemplative and silent time with God into your busy life?

Chapter 2

AND JESUS CALLED HIM SIMON PETER

I NEARLY GOT ARRESTED AND thrown into the slammer for what I thought was an innocuous incident at an art gallery in Washington, DC. The police thought otherwise. My crime? I got too close to a sculpture on display and didn't adhere to the posted warning signs that informed me I was venturing into the territory of an art thief. When I set off the alarm, the rest of my day went south very fast.

The policeman entrusted with protecting these precious works of ingenuity and craftsmanship was as hot under the collar as a tin barn on the Fourth of July. Of that, I was sure from his vocal inflection and the less-than-grandiose statements he mouthed about me to his peers from his radio.

My first instinct was to let my flesh take over and tell ol' Roscoe P. Coletrain, "Yeah, buddy; this is the crime I've been planning all my life: setting off an alarm in an art gallery! It's right up there with jumping over the turnstile on the Metro so I don't have to pay."

The Holy Spirit, however, was interceding to the Father on my behalf at that exact moment. As a result, I could only muster the words, "I'm sorry, officer. I didn't realize I had gotten that close to the sculpture. It won't happen again." I chose my words wisely on that day, and my freedom as a civilian continued because of them.

There is a sculpture in the Bible I get close to and look at quite often because I am amazed at the masterpiece the Divine Sculptor crafted with His heavenly chisel. That sculpture goes by the name of Simon Peter.

Peter means "rock" in the language of the New Testament,[8] which is ironic because he acts more like sinking sand when he first appears in the Gospels. But when Peter answered Jesus' call to follow Him, God changed him into something special so that he could touch other people's lives. He turned him into a man of faith, whose confession of Christ was as strong as the massive fitted stone blocks in the towers of Jerusalem that stood in his day.

Peter wasn't satisfied with just observing Jesus from the parade route. He wanted to follow Him inside the tent with all of his heart, soul, and mind. What came out the exit door was genuinely remarkable and miraculous.

CHALKSTONE PETER

In the Book of Acts, Peter preaches with resolute conviction (2:14-41 and 4:8-1) and behaves with visceral courage (4:18-20). But when we meet him in the Gospels, Peter was as brittle as chalkstone both emotionally and spiritually. He looked solid on the outside but crumbled under the slightest bit of pressure. Matthew tells us, "As Jesus was walking beside the Sea of Galilee, he saw two brothers, Simon called Peter and his brother Andrew. They were casting a net into the lake, for they were fishermen. 'Come, follow me,' Jesus said, 'and I will send you out to fish for people.' <u>At once</u> they left their nets and followed him" (Matt. 4:18-20—emphasis mine).

In his grand entrance into the pages of Holy Writ, Peter already demonstrates how acting on impulse came quite naturally. In this case, though, it helped guide him to make the right decision. From the Greek a*koloutheo*, "to follow" here indicates commitment and cost.[9] Peter was well aware that his decision to leave his fishing hole and follow Jesus might break him financially. Operating on the fly, not with forethought, came naturally to him. As a result, he chose wisely to do it.

Not all of his impulsive decisions turned out so well, however. Matthew narrated a foolish one the first time he wrote a first-person account of any disciple:

> Shortly before dawn Jesus went out to them, walking on the lake. When the disciples saw him walking on the lake, they were terrified. "It's a ghost," they said, and cried out in fear. But Jesus immediately said to them: "Take courage! It is I. Don't be afraid." "Lord, if it's you," Peter replied, "tell me to come to you on the water." "Come," he said. Then Peter got down out of the boat, walked on water and came toward Jesus. But when he saw the wind, he was afraid and, beginning to sink, cried out, "Lord, save me!" Immediately Jesus reached out his hand and caught him. "You of little faith," he said, "why did you doubt?" (Matt. 14:25-31).

Notice Matthew's detail in his recording of Peter's lack of faith. He got out of the boat on a whim and nearly drowned. Here, his impulsiveness stymies his faith instead of fostering it. It's one of his main character hiccups. He wasn't quite ready spiritually for the water-walk. Consequently, his impulse to do it nearly killed him.

FIRST TO FOLLOW AND FIRST TO FLEE

As a result, Peter is usually the first to follow and the first to flee. We can see this most clearly in his conversation with Jesus in the Upper Room Discourse:

> Then Jesus told them, "This very night you will all fall away on account of me, for it is written: 'I will strike the shepherd, and the sheep of the flock will be scattered.' But after I have risen, I will go ahead of you into Galilee. Peter replied, "Even if all fall away on account of you, I never will." "Truly I tell you," Jesus answered, "This very night, before the rooster crows, you will disown me three times." But Peter declared, "Even if I have to die with you, I will never disown you." And all the other disciples said the same (Matt. 26:31-35).

You know the story well, I'm sure. Just a taste of persecution similar to what Jesus had to endure was enough for Peter to deny him three times and bolt for safety faster than a mule runs while eating briars. He crumbled in the palm of suffering like chalkstone. The moment Peter's faith was going to cost him something, he was nowhere to be found.

Before we go slinging mud on Peter, we should note Matthew's comment at the end of the passage. Except for John, every disciple abandoned Jesus. Following and fleeing came automatically to them as well because they, too, were chalkstone. Peter's impulses were just archetypical of the rest of the disciples. Out of all the impulsive disciples, Simon Peter's impetuous actions were chosen by Matthew to show his readers the problems they can create if they are not surrendered to Christ.

FALSE SPIRITUAL CONFIDENCE

I have never in my life named anyone Satan for using foolish statements in church, even though I probably should have. Peter, though, has the rare distinction among all of the disciples, except Judas Iscariot, of being referred to in precisely this manner. He didn't like Jesus predicting His death, so he let our Lord know about it. The Almighty's response was unexpected, yet appropriate: "But when Jesus turned and looked at his disciples, he rebuked Peter. 'Get behind me, Satan!' he said. 'You do not have in mind the concerns of God, but merely human concerns'" (Mark 8:33).

In the first century Jewish mind, a Messiah Who would be rejected by their leaders was inconceivable. Their concept of messianic hope was a political one that included liberation from their enemies and a restoration of the glory Israel shared among the nations when David and Solomon were kings. Jesus certainly was going to liberate His people and establish a kingdom, but not in the way they were thinking. As a result, Peter impulsively and unwisely decided to educate God the Son about it.

You would expect that he learned to be quiet after this. He couldn't master the taming of the tongue, though. In the next chapter, Mark tells us:

> After six days Jesus took Peter, James and John with him and led them up a high mountain, where they were all alone. There he was transfigured before them. His clothes became dazzling white, whiter than anyone in the world could bleach them. And there appeared before them Elijah and Moses, who were talking with Jesus. Peter said to Jesus, "Rabbi, it is good for us to be here. Let us put up three shelters—one for you, one for Moses and one for Elijah." (He did not know what to say, they were so frightened). Then a cloud appeared and covered them, and a <u>voice came from the cloud</u>: "This is my Son, whom I love. Listen to him" (Mark 9:2-7—emphasis mine).

Peter now owned another unique distinction: he's the only person recorded in the Bible rebuked by God from a cloud! Ouch! The last time a cloud was this active in biblical history, it was guiding the children of Israel to the Promised Land (Exod. 40:38). In light of this, Peter should have silenced the aperture responsible verbal communication and understood that a new exodus was about to take place. Instead, he felt inclined to educate God in the flesh AGAIN about the significance of the occasion. As a result, the God of the Exodus intervened from a cloud above to quiet him.

Had Peter tried to exit stage left and go back to what he knew best—fishing with his mouth shut and his nets open—no one could have blamed him. But Jesus had other plans for him.

He could have brooded about the rebukes like Judas Iscariot, but he didn't. He could have separated from the other disciples after his third denial, but he was there among them (John 21:2). Though his impulsivity and spiritual pomposity were glaring character weaknesses, Peter's desire to please his Master was his greatest strength. As a result, the Master Sculptor chiseled away the former in light of the latter. Simon Peter continued to journey inside the tent, albeit with a spiritual limp. And that decision to keep following Jesus was all his Master needed to craft him into the leader he wanted Peter to be.

CLAYSTONE PETER

Because it has not yet fossilized, claystone molds easily in the palm of your hand. Of all his qualities, Peter's teachable spirit and ability to learn from his mistakes are his noblest. Without these, God had no *petras* (stone) to mold.

Solomon observed, "Whoever disregards discipline comes to poverty and shame, but whoever heeds correction is honored" (Prov. 13:18). Judas was reduced to shame because he couldn't accept instruction. God honored Peter because he was claystone that could.

TEACHABLE SPIRIT

On many occasions in the Gospels, Peter took the initiative during a teachable moment to seek more instruction from Jesus when the rest of the disciples remained silent. He desired to learn from his Master about what's Divine and consistent with God's character:

1. "Lord, if it's you . . . tell me to come to you on the water" (Matt. 14:28).

2. "Explain the parable to us" (Matt. 15:15).

3. "Lord, how many times shall I forgive my brother or sister who sins against me? Up to seven times?" (Matt. 18:21).

4. "Rabbi, look! The fig tree you cursed has withered" (Mark 11:21).

5. "Tell us [Peter, James, John, and Andrew], when will these things happen? And what will be the sign that they are all about to be fulfilled?" (Mark 13:3-4).

6. "Master, we've worked hard all night and haven't caught anything. But because you say so, I will let down the nets" (Luke 5:5).

7. "Lord, are you telling this parable to us, or to everyone?" (Luke 12:41).

8. "We have left all we had to follow you" (Luke 18:28).

9. "Lord, to whom shall we go? You have the words of eternal life" (John 6:68).

10. "Lord, are you going to wash my feet" (John 13:6).

11. "Ask [Jesus] which one he means" (John 13:24).

Jesus can work with and through a disciple with a curious spirit so long as he is teachable. Peter was. His openness to instruction guided his hands into the protective yoke of the love of Christ, regardless of the cost or risk—a trait he observed from his Master.

The disciples were spooked when they saw Jesus walking on water. Peter wasn't; he got out of the boat, even though he sunk like a sack of hammers (Matt. 14:30). But at least he didn't drop under the water without trying! Such an attitude counts mightily in the economy of God, much more than that of those arrested so much by fear that they never even attempt a boat exodus. Peter did; he was honored by God for it, too, though he lacked the water-walking faith he needed to keep him upright at that moment.

LEARNING FROM MISTAKES

Peter's spirit was willing, but his flesh was weak (Matt. 26:41). He was utterly powerless to overcome his impulsiveness in his own strength. Matthew gives us proof in his narrative of what happened after Peter stuck his foot in his mouth during Jesus' transfiguration: "When the disciples [Peter, James, and John)] heard this, they fell facedown to the ground, terrified. But Jesus came and touched them. 'Get up,' he said. 'Don't be afraid'" (Matt. 17:6-7).

In this salient biblical event, where the disciples witnessed the majesty of Christ only to have it followed up by Peter's foolish comments, we get a glimpse of what changed Peter and the rest of the disciples: the unmerited favor of God when it's least deserved. Peter should have been consumed by fire for misspeaking. He certainly earned it. Jesus touched him instead.

Let that sink in for a second. When Peter deserved and expected judgment, the kindness of God enveloped him. Only the Lord's kindness could lead to his transformation and resoluteness to become a fisher of men. And that kindness was demonstrated on the Mount of Transfiguration through a criticism, a healing touch, and two gentle commands.

God's reproof demonstrated His holiness; His touch exhibited His restoration. Peter learned to balance both of these attributes of God's character after the ascension while preaching at Pentecost: "Peter replied, 'Repent and be baptized, every one of you, in the name of Jesus Christ for the forgiveness of your sins. And you will receive the gift of the Holy Spirit. The promise is for you and your children and for all who are far off—for all whom the Lord our God will call'" (Acts 2:38-39—emphasis mine).

We church folk usually prefer one attribute of God's character over the other. Those who, unlike Peter, tolerate their demons instead of asking God for help in casting them out will quarantine His grace from His holiness. On the other hand, those who judge people by a standard they do not keep will often pontificate about God's *holy standards* because they are consumed by the guilt of not keeping them.

Peter learned this discipleship lesson through experience, not a theology book. Such wisdom would have been impossible to gain had he stayed at the base of the mountain, inside the boat, and outside the tent of discipleship, oblivious to his personal need for Christ to quiet his soul.

LIMESTONE PETER

Because it is unyielding and not easily moved, limestone is one of the strongest rocks on Earth. Try breaking it with your hands, and you'll instantly regret it. Reducing this type of stone to rubble under pressure is virtually impossible. That is what Peter eventually became: unyielding and immovable. Two episodes contributed mightily to his fossilization: his confession and commission.

HIS CONFESSION

Though he liked to pontificate without thinking, Peter was capable of internal processing. He witnessed Jesus feed five thousand people with a few loaves of bread and a couple of fish. On another occasion, he witnessed Jesus feed four thousand (Matt. 16:9-10). These miracles didn't go unnoticed by the Galileans who witnessed them either. Jesus, already aware they were prating about Who He was, had a conversation with Peter about it:

> "But what about you," he asked. "Who do you say I am?" Simon Peter answered, "You are the Messiah, the Son of the living God." Jesus replied, "Blessed are you, Simon son of Jonah, for this was not revealed to you by flesh and blood, but by my Father in heaven. And I tell you that you are Peter, and on this rock I will build my church, and the gates of Hades will not overcome it" (Matt. 16:15-18).

In the Scriptures, when God began a new work in someone, He often changed their name. He changed *Abram*, whose name meant "exalted father," to *Abraham*, meaning "the father of many," after His covenant with him (Gen. 17:5).[10] He changed *Jacob's* name from "cheat," which is what he was, to *Israel*, meaning "overcomer," when he finally decided to stop deceiving others and start telling the truth (Gen. 32:28).[11] Luke shifted the emphasis from the persecuting *Saul* to the graceful *Paul* after he began his ministry to the Gentiles as a follower of Jesus with a radically new life mission and focus (Acts 9:1-19).

El Shaddai (the Lord Almighty) does this because He is the Lord. His name doesn't change; it stays the same "yesterday, today, and forever" (Heb. 13:8). Though our names may not change, our stories do quite frequently because we are not perfect. When God interrupts our story to tell a different one—as

He did with those above—then we begin to understand what He's up to in the world. He crafts us into new creations so that we can be suitable ambassadors of His covenant (2 Cor. 5:17-21). That's how a *cheat* became an *overcomer* and a *Saul* became a *Paul*. And that is indeed how a *Simon* became a *Peter*. Faith became his victory to conquer his world.[12] Consequently, the name shift indicated God's graceful purpose in his life would prevail, even though *Peter* would fail miserably again.

HIS COMMISSION

My favorite story about Peter happens after he failed miserably. The resurrected Jesus sought him out on the shores of the Sea of Galilee because Peter denied Him the last time he saw the Lord. What followed was a tri-fold commission:

> When they had finished eating, Jesus said to Simon Peter, "Simon son of John, do you love me more than these?" "Yes, Lord," he said, "you know that I love you." Jesus said, "Feed my lambs." Again Jesus said, "Simon son of John, do you love me?" "Yes, Lord, you know that I love you." Jesus said, "Take care of my sheep." The third time he said to him, "Simon son of John, do you love me?" Peter was hurt because Jesus asked him the third time, "Do you love me?" He said, "Lord, you know all things; you know that I love you." Jesus said, "Feed my sheep" (John 21:15-17).

Tri-fold patterns that move a narrative or prophetic utterance are not uncommon in the Scriptures. They are rhetorical strategies biblical writers and speakers employ to denote completeness.

In his plea for Judah to avoid the mistakes of the Northern Kingdom, Hosea condemned her (1) prophets, (2) priests, and (3) kings (Hosea 4:4-5; 5:1). Elijah doused his sacrifice with water three times on Mount Carmel (1 Kings 18:33-35). After he called down the fire from heaven, it (1) burned the wood, (2) burned the stones and soil, and (3) "licked up the water in the trench" (1 Kings 18:38).

Similarly, the tri-fold commission Peter received from the Lord was complete because it was (1) lovingly confrontational about his sin, (2) restorative of their relationship, and (3) truthful about his future. Peter would teach the Gospel he learned from Jesus; he would die for it also, just like his Master. With these words, the transformation into limestone was complete. That's why he became an exemplar of Christian courage and a living illustration of the humility from God after the Ascension.

AN EXEMPLAR OF CHRISTIAN COURAGE

According to Luke, the Sanhedrin, the highest Jewish court in the land, arrested Peter and John for preaching Jesus to a lame man miraculously healed by God. When the Sanhedrin asked them to cease (Acts 4:1-7), *Simon* would have obliged during Passion Week. But *Peter* would not:

> "Rulers and elders of the people! If we are being called to account today for an act of kindness shown to a man who was lame and are being asked how he was healed, then know this, you and all the people of Israel: It is by the name of Jesus Christ of Nazareth, whom you crucified but whom God raised from the dead, that this man stands before you healed. Jesus is 'the stone you builders rejected,' which has become the cornerstone. Salvation is found in no one else, for there is no other name under heaven given to mankind by which we must be saved" (Acts 4:8-12).

And that courage in the face of danger produced this reaction: "When they saw the courage of Peter and John and realized that they were unschooled, ordinary men, they were astonished and they took note that these men had been with Jesus" (Acts 4:13).

In the language of the New Testament, the word *astonished* denotes the idea of being "amazed to the level of wonder."[13] Peter had been a coward the last time he ran into these officials. So, they were floored to observe their courage when faced with great danger on this occasion—Peter especially.

Jesus wasn't. He had molded Peter (and John as well) into limestone long before that moment. Jesus took broken vessels and crafted them into witnesses who desired to do what was right even if it wasn't popular. He still crafts leaders much the same way. And refusing to be content with observing Jesus from the parade route and choosing to follow Him inside the tent is what led to that transformation in Peter's life.

A LIVING ILLUSTRATION OF THE HUMILITY FROM GOD

Examine great leaders, and you will find that humility is a defining hallmark of each one. How they developed it depends to a certain degree on how they responded to life experiences, particularly challenging ones. Peter arrived via failure and getting back up off the mat. That's why we should listen to him when he implores us, "Clothe yourselves with humility toward one another, because, 'God opposes the proud but shows favor to the humble.' Humble yourselves, therefore, under God's mighty hand, that he may lift you up in due time" (1 Peter 5:5-6).

Dependence and submission to something more significant than you are indeed prerequisites for genuine humility. That something is Christ. Peter learned both by observing Jesus. John, the son of Zebedee, did also, as we shall see. We practice what we watch from our examples, and Peter called his readers to follow Christ's model. We are called to wear humility like we're adorning Versace or Polo. Such a lowly display mobilizes us to love God, neighbor, and self in a way that is consistent with His Divine character.

Yes, my friends. I almost got taken to the reformatory clink in Washington, DC, for getting too close to a sculpture made and chiseled by human hands. But I am learning in my times on the mountain with God that I can never get close enough to the Divine sculpture that is *Simon Peter*. As a matter of fact, the closer I examine that work of art that God created, the more I want my heavenly Michelangelo to craft me the same way. What about you?

SOME QUESTIONS TO PONDER BEFORE MOVING ON

1. Read 1 Peter 3:18. How can choosing to live in victory—not defeat—lead to being alive in the Spirit of God? How does unforgiveness of self or others point to spiritual immaturity in our lives?

2. How have you grown from your mistakes? How have they made you stronger?

3. Read Proverbs 9:8. How does a proud person respond to constructive criticism? What about a wise person? What is the difference between the two in terms of their spirit? How will you react to appropriate criticism in light of what you have learned about Peter?

Chapter 3

JAMES, SON OF ZEBEDEE, AND THE GOSPEL EXCHANGE

WE HUMANS ARE AN ANGRY lot, I assure you. Don't believe me? Wait three hundred hours for a parking space at Walmart only to have someone cut you off and slide right into it. You'll find my observation credible then. Or get a note from the Internal Revenue Service advising you to phone them to discuss your tax assessment. And when you do, you learn quickly that you probably have a better chance of finding Elvis Presley or Jimmy Hoffa alive than you do of talking to an actual human being in that organization. That will make you—as we say where I'm from—"see red" really fast.

Better yet, spend a whole day cleaning and mopping floors in your house and then watch your benevolence-lacking adolescent male create mud art on them because he forgot to wipe his feet when sneaking into the house after curfew. If that ever happens to you, I will put safe money on the fact that you might "see red" and have a coronary at the same time!

I told you, we who reside right here on this Earth are an incensed assemblage. Being outraged is innate in each of us, especially when we are put off by someone or something. But I doubt very seriously that anyone would take the time to craft a nickname for you when you "see red." Not unless, of course, you've developed patterns others have noticed that are toxic and dangerous enough to label you as such.

Jesus, however, had one for two brothers specifically because of their explosive anger and penchant for "seeing red" quite easily. They were James and John, the sons of Zebedee. But Jesus called them *Boanerges*, meaning "sons of thunder" (Mark 3:17).

A SON OF THUNDER

An Aramaic epithet, *Boanerges* denotes the idea that James and John expressed their umbrage in a passionate and overly zealous way. It comes from two Hebrew roots: *ben*, meaning "sons," and *regesh*, meaning "thunder, or quaking." So transliterated, the epithet means, "sons of (the) quaking (heavens)."[14]

Thunder can denote the voice of God in the Scriptures (Exod. 9:23; Psalm 29:3). Jesus uses it in the nickname, however, to convey these brother's emotional makeup. They were quick-tempered, indignant, and authoritarian; traits we see clearly on one occasion in Luke's Gospel (Luke 9:54).[15] When they "saw red," they had no trouble "bringing the thunder."

When the Israelites looked up at Mount Sinai and saw thunder and lightning, they trembled and stood at a distance (Exod. 20:18). When Hannah dedicated her son, Samuel, to the Lord for His purposes, she asked God to shatter those who would contend against Him with thunder from the heavens (1 Sam. 2:10). Had you gotten on the wrong side of James and John, though, they would have had no trouble trying to crush you with a barrage of verbal insults.

They were passionate individuals who were radically committed to proclaiming what they thought was right, regardless of the consequences. Because both nature and nurture hardwired them as such, anger and condemnation awaited those who challenged James and John. They were full-fledged anger addicts and proud of it.

A SON OF ZEBEDEE

You will have a hard time finding James referenced in the Gospels apart from his brother, John. And you will face an even stiffer challenge trying to isolate both of them from their father. The Gospel writers wanted their readers to know that Zebedee was a mover and shaker in that region of Galilee near Capernaum. For example, in the first Gospel in our New Testament, James and John are not referenced by Matthew apart from their father, Zebedee:

1. "Going on from there, he saw two brothers, James <u>son of Zebedee</u> and his brother John. They were in a boat <u>with their father Zebedee</u>, preparing their nets. Jesus called them, and immediately they left the boat <u>and their father</u> and followed him" (Matt. 4:21-22—emphasis mine).

2. "These are the names of the twelve apostles: first Simon (who is called Peter) and his brother Andrew; <u>James son of Zebedee, and his brother John</u>" (Matt. 10:2—emphasis mine).

3. "Then the <u>mother of Zebedee's sons</u> came to Jesus with her sons and, kneeling down, asked a favor of him" (Matt. 20:20—emphasis mine).

4. "He took Peter and the two sons of Zebedee along with him, and he began to be sorrowful and troubled" (Matt. 26:37).

5. "Many women were there, watching from a distance. They had followed Jesus from Galilee to care for his needs. Among them were Mary Magdalene, Mary the mother of James and Joseph, and the mother <u>of Zebedee's sons</u>" (Matt. 27:55-56—emphasis mine).

Though referring to someone with the introductory "son of" was common in antiquity, the way Matthew speaks of Zebedee and his sons is noteworthy. He phrases the first example in a way that suggests Zebedee was a fisherman with some financial means.[16] Notice also the order of Matthew's narrative pertaining to what James and John had to do to follow Jesus: leave the "boat" (a financial implication) with their "father" (a familial implication) on it. And he informs us of this *twice* in consecutive sentences. That's important information—perhaps also the reason their mother asked for a personal favor relating to her sons in the second reference.

Furthermore, we can also conclude from the fourth example that Matthew can refer to James and John without even using their names, only Zebedee's, because he assumed his readers would know which disciples he was talking about because of who their father was in the Galilean region of which Matthew himself worked. The redeemed tax collector uses similar language about their mother also in example three.

Therefore, we can rightly assume that when James and John decided to follow Jesus, they had to literally count the cost. And if you combine their familial prestige with their emotional outbursts of anger, you have a recipe for disaster: a type of religion that scars people for life on the receiving end of it. That was the road James and John were heading down had they stayed the course.

But they didn't. Jesus intervened by calling them out of the boat. They only had to believe. Doing so required a life exchange: the one James and John had planned for themselves, paved with a trust fund not contingent on completing anger management classes, for the one that Jesus had purposed for them.

The Lord wanted James and his brother to understand how truthfulness, personal devotion, and ethical praxis relate to each other. He wanted them to learn that God did not send their Caller into the world to condemn it (John 3:17). He sent Him to save it instead (John 3:16).

Such an exchange did not take place in the life of Zebedee's sons by watching Jesus from the parade route. It happened when they became pupils of Jesus inside the tent of discipleship. And because they did, their whole life story became a living illustration of the Gospel of God.

EXCHANGING SELF-PRESERVATION FOR A PERSON

We all have a tremendous need for self-preservation. James and his brother were no different. Trading their trust fund for Divine tutoring would have been a sour pill to swallow for both of them.

The rich, young ruler couldn't make that exchange (Luke 18:18-30). James and John could and did. When their Master called from the shores of the Sea of Galilee and asked for their lives, they followed with two actions. First, James and John left their fishing boat *immediately* (Matt. 4:22). Such a move means they relinquished their commitment to the family business—and all the spoils that came with it—for Christ the moment He called them.

Before He did, the brothers were mending their nets (Matt. 4:21). They weren't small ones either. Each one they patched had five parts to it that were over one hundred feet long.[17] The Zebedee Family Fishing Company had the seafood market cornered in Galilee. They had more nets than most, and Zebedee's boats were even equipped for cooking during all-night fishing expeditions because of his successful business endeavors in the region.[18]

Second, James and his brother left their father in the boat to follow Jesus (Matt. 4:22). According to Mark, Zebedee hired day laborers to work for him (Mark 1:20). His wife, Salome, was very generous with the family fortune as well (Mark 15:40-41). Perhaps that helps explain why John was allowed by Caiaphas the High Priest to follow Jesus into the temple courtyard in Jerusalem to face the Sanhedrin, which was something Peter couldn't do.

Zebedee and his family were high society Galileans known well by the Jerusalem elite. Zebedee even helped fund the synagogue in Capernaum, where he lived. A pillar from it states, "Alphaeus, the son of Zebedee, the son of John, made this column. May it be for him a blessing."[19]

When a need arose, Zebedee was the individual who stroked a check and dispatched helping hands. He was not God in the flesh, though. According to Jesus, "Anyone who loves their father or mother more than me is not worthy of me; anyone who loves their son or daughter more than me is not worthy of me. Whoever does not take up their cross and follow me is not worthy of me. Whoever finds their life will lose it, and whoever loses their life for my sake will find it" (Matt. 10:37-39).

James didn't need a seminary-trained theologian to help him understand the essence of those words. He was a living illustration of what they meant. Jesus demanded this son of Zebedee's heart; James, therefore, gave it to Him.

When it comes to Jesus' mission in the world to reign in the hearts of His people, He will share His glory with no one. Zebedee learned that the hard way the moment he saw the bottoms of his sons' feet leaving his boat.

All the wealth in the world and his father's ability to influence others could not have taught James that he was dead in his transgressions without Christ (Eph. 2:1). Neither could they inform him that silver spoons and tongues don't belong in the same sentence with God. Only Jesus could teach him those lessons. Christ alone was the only one qualified to teach James that he needed to learn that wealth and wrath form a cocktail of religious poison if not tamed.

Without this exchange, there is no Gospel. The issue here is not whether we will exchange our financial future for missions. It's would we if Jesus called us to do it? Are we willing to give Jesus those things in our lives that could become idols if left un-surrendered to His Lordship? That is—and always will be—the issue.

The moment they left the boat, the "Thunder Brothers" put their lives into the hands of the One Who created them. Zebedee and Salome probably had big plans for their progeny. Jesus did, too—just not in the way the "First Fishing Family of Galilee" intended.

EXCHANGING PRESTIGE FOR THE PASSION OF THE CHRIST

In spite of their differences, all of the disciples not named Judas Iscariot had one thing in common: Jesus marched them purposely to and "through the valley of the shadow of death" (Psalm 23:4), so they would recognize He was with them and would never forsake them (Heb. 13:5). He pruned them all with pain to make them suitable vessels for the Gospel. To use them mightily, Jesus had to wound them deeply.

Even for the privileged brothers, the cross had to come before exaltation. Neither understood this at first, nor did their mother:

> Then the mother of Zebedee's sons came to Jesus with her sons and, kneeling down, asked a favor of him. "What is it you want?" he asked. She said, "Grant that one of these two sons of mine may sit at your right and the other at your left in your kingdom." "You don't know what you are asking," Jesus said to them. "Can you drink the cup I am going to drink?" "We can," they answered (Matt. 20:20-22).

Salome thought her boys deserved prestige in the economy of the Kingdom of God because of who her husband was. Her boys did, too, but preferred to let Salome Zebedee do their talking. She got straight to the point by asking Jesus to elevate her children to the most distinguished positions in His kingdom.

Sitting at the right hand of a monarch was the highest place of honor for a person of importance in Israel. When Bathsheba, King Solomon's mother, approached her son to speak favorably of Adonijah, she sat at his right hand (1 Kings 2:19). Those of the second highest importance in the king's court got reserved seats on the left side of the monarch. Abner, for example, sat to the left of King Saul because he captained his army, according to the Jewish historian Flavius Josephus.[20]

Such a pompous and entitled request implies that Salome and her offspring wanted to use Jesus for the glory and honor of the Zebedee family. He was their ticket to further vainglory. Had they taken the spoons out of their mouths and thought before speaking, they would have recognized that asking Jesus for this type of favor was a dangerous path to tread. Violating the

Lord's command to not use His name for vain purposes (Exod. 20:7) would have surely followed had Jesus granted Salome's request.

As human beings, we want to feel appreciated and gain the approval of others. We are also inclined to parlay our connections to win influence and power. But if that is what drives us in our relationship with Jesus as His disciples—to use His name to further our agenda—then no exchange has taken place.

Salome did not understand this; neither did James and John. They wanted the glory of the kingdom without the cross of Christ. They needed to learn that to become great in His kingdom, they had to become the least (Matt. 20:26). And to be exalted in His economy, they had to become humble (Matt. 23:12). And Jesus' subtle rebuke in His answer to Salome's question was the first step in that direction.

The Zebedee family sure had a lot to learn. Jesus, however, was eager and willing to teach them because, by faith alone, they kept marching into the tent of discipleship in spite of the rebuke. And there, inside that providential place of learning to be God's people in the world, James, John, and Salome would learn to see people—even those who are hostile to the Gospel—through the gentle, yet truthful, eyes of God.

EXCHANGING PUNISHMENT FOR PARDON

Beginning in chapter nine, verse fifty-one, Luke narrated the start of Jesus' death march to Jerusalem. It was a journey to the cross, a journey of death that had to precede resurrection and exaltation. This physician, missionary, and Gospel writer also informs us that Jesus sent messengers ahead of Him to proclaim the Good News to those along the route. The "Thunder Brothers" were part of that convoy (Luke 9:52). Imagine them thinking, *We are on a mission from God. If anybody disagrees with us or rejects the message we've been divinely dispatched to tell, we can call thunder and fire down from Heaven as Elijah did. It worked for him; it will work for us. God will hear us and oblige because He is on our side.*

They traveled through Samaria, which, to their credit, shows a mustard seed of faith because devout Jews in those days would not set foot on Samaritan soil. They hated the Samaritans for many reasons. First and foremost, they were half-Jewish and half-Assyrian. When the Assyrians seized Samaria in 722 BC, they took up residence alongside the Jews there and intermarried with them, something the Old Covenant people of God were not supposed to do (Deut. 7:3).

Second, orthodox Jews, regardless of the sectarian designation (Pharisee, Sadducee, Herodian, Essene, etc.), viewed them as apostates for having the audacity to suggest Moses received the law on Mount Gerizim, not Mount Sinai (John 4:20). To make matters worse, they rejected all but the first five books of the Old Testament.

The straightest and shortest route from Galilee to Jerusalem was straight through Samaria. Jews in the first century, though, weren't interested in walking the shortest path if that meant walking through that place they had a hard time speaking audibly by its proper name. They just went around it instead. All, of course, except the Twelve, in light of Jesus' command.

When they strolled into town reluctantly, they, much like Jonah to the Assyrians, begrudgingly heralded the news of the long-awaited Kingdom of God. They got their pride wounded, however, when those already undesirable folks had no interest in listening to them and told them to take a hike. Such a rejection prompted this question from the thunder duo: "Lord, do you want us to call fire down from heaven to destroy them?" (Luke 9:54).

James and his brother were thunderous about biblical truth. Unlike the Samaritans, they believed the whole Old Testament was the Word of God. They also believed Jesus was the Messiah. Not the Samaritans, though. They wanted absolutely nothing to do with Him or them. When they got rejected by the group of people who wouldn't have even had the privilege of being picked last at a first-century Jewish pickup basketball game, the thunder-tongued siblings wanted Jesus' permission to destroy them. But notice how the Lord responded: "Jesus turned and rebuked them" (Luke 9:55).

Our Lord had just finished rebuking the disciples (Luke 9:46-48) for arguing about who was the best at "standing up for Jesus."[21] Now James and John feel the sting of a Divine rebuke aimed directly at them for misunderstanding their Savior's mission in the world. Jesus the Christ came to offer the world clemency and mercy, not thunder and lightning. Those forces of holy wrath were reserved for Jesus, and Jesus alone, on the cross, not for those of Samaritan blood, or even for John and James, who, like Elijah, wanted God to act according to their script and at their beckoning.

Isn't it interesting that Jesus saves His reprimand, not for the Samaritans who scoffed at His Gospel and His people, but for these brothers because they did not understand the New Covenant? It's about turning the other cheek (Matt. 5:39) and not counting trespasses (2 Cor. 5:19). It's about pardon when punishment is deserved (Luke 18:13). It's about proclaiming the Gospel and having enough faith to let that Providential—and, therefore, always relevant—message stand alone without threat or manipulation from the clay jars who deliver it. Most of all, it's about trusting the Holy Spirit to do the changing and convicting, not us (John 16:8).

According to Solomon, "Those who disregard discipline despise themselves, but the one who heeds correction gains understanding" (Prov. 15:32).

Correcting James and John for living in the wrong covenant was instrumental in helping both of them recover from their "Wrath Toward Others Addiction" and grow from it. He admired their passion for what is truthful, right, and noble. Why wouldn't He? He created them in His image with those virtues. That's what made them tick after all. But on this day, they learned humility and compassion through two rebukes divinely given to calm the river of conflict inside their souls—both of which they would need in their future missional Gospel endeavors.

Condemnation was not their job, nor is it ours. It's God's. He—and He alone—is holy and just. Our job is to announce the truth without compromise and dress it in a way that demonstrates love and compassion for the listener. Both go together. That's the New Covenant. Emphasize one without the other, and you speak falsely and lead people astray. Both go hand in hand. James and John learned that; so should we.

EXCHANGING POWER FOR EMPOWERMENT

History is replete with folks whose lust for power and influence led to their demise. In the latter part of the nineteenth century, Thomas Nast's drawings in *Harper's Weekly* exposed William "Boss" Tweed, the behemoth New York political parasite eventually convicted in 1877 for stealing millions of taxpayer's monies.[22]

Recently and unfortunately, the architect of the conservative movement within my Christian denomination, Dr. Paige Patterson, was removed as president of Southwestern Baptist Theological Seminary for his role in covering up sexual abuse.[23] Instead of protecting the defenseless, he thought it best to bulwark the organization. That only hurt it, and now he will have an asterisk next to his name in the annals of Baptist history.

These things happen because, as John Dalberg-Action said correctly, "Power tends to corrupt and absolute power corrupts absolutely."[24] A dastardly fate of this kind could have easily awaited James had he become head of the Zebedee empire. He could have even figured out how to parlay his penchant for stepping on people who crossed him into even higher power and influence than his father had. But James did not. He cared more about being empowered by God than continuing in the family business or even attempting to vainly exploit Jesus for his benefit.

On forty-six occasions in the Book of Acts, the Holy Spirit empowered the disciples to build the Kingdom of God, including James. Unlike Boss Tweed, James' capacitation would lead to spiritual life for other people when

God's mission in the world became his (Acts 1:8). He faithfully preached the truth with compassion for his listeners in Jerusalem. That Gospel exchange cost James his life. According to Luke, "It was about this time that King Herod [Agrippa] arrested some who belonged to the church, intending to persecute them. He had James, brother of John, put to death with the sword" (Acts 12:1-2). The cross came before exaltation quite literally for him. He was the only apostle, besides Judas Iscariot, with a death record in the New Testament.

He is in Heaven with Jesus, and you read about him in the Bible today because he went inside the tent and learned from Jesus. In that beautiful place of discipleship and fellowship, James exchanged his life for the privilege "to know Christ—yes, to know the power of his resurrection and participation in is sufferings, becoming like him in his death" (Phil. 3:10).

That was the Gospel then. That is the Gospel now. That Gospel comes by faith alone and bears spiritual fruit in our lives when we exchange our life plans for His, regardless of where that road leads.

SOME QUESTIONS TO PONDER BEFORE MOVING ON

1. Read Ephesians 4:26. What is the best way to deal with anger according to the text?

2. I often get frustrated when people benefit from wickedness. Read Psalm 37:5-9. What is the best way to curb frustration that can lead to anger according to the text?

3. Vengeance implies condemnation. Read Romans 8:1. How might fellow believers paint a false picture of the character of God when they get angry to the point of condemning?

Chapter 4
JOHN, THE DISCIPLE JESUS LOVED

MY APARTMENT BATHROOM MIRROR OBSERVED numerous mock church interviews during my seminary days. I stood in front of it for hours polishing my testimony of salvation and call to ministry. To this day, I value that mirror because it got the chance to witness something that others only sporadically get to see: Derrick dressed up in unwrinkled attire. What a rare sight!

What it never viewed, however, were iterated responses to queries about my "greatest character strengths." I knew prospective church leaders wanted to hear what I thought about my assets. I just dreaded the subject matter because it made me uncomfortable.

I cannot recall the specifics of my self-evaluation in those interviews. Be assured, though, that when inquisitors asked me the incommodious character question, the thought never occurred to me to respond with these words: "I think my greatest character strength would undoubtedly be my humility."

Two commonly used words in the English Language derive from the Latin word *humilis,* meaning, "low: humble and humility."[25] When using them to paint a picture of personal character, these words are the slipperiest of virtues. For the moment you congratulate yourself for possessing them is the instant you dispose of them!

Phillips Brooks, the great Episcopalian preacher of the nineteenth century, once proclaimed: "The true way to be humble is not to stoop till you are smaller than yourself, but to stand at your real height against some higher nature."[26]

When we stop comparing ourselves to others and start evaluating our lives relative to the infinite height of Jesus, we begin to learn Christian humility. It does not imply we hate ourselves; humility is instead standing tall in His grace while continually looking up for guidance and provision.

John, the other son of Zebedee, exemplified this type of humility—the kind that leads to spiritual wisdom. Though he was born with a silver spoon and fiery tongue in his mouth, John humbled himself the moment he left his father's boat to follow Jesus. He continued to do so for the rest of his life. As a result, he gained wisdom which stands out in the New Testament in its form and depth of reflection. Consequently, we can learn much about how humility produces Divine wisdom from John's sterling example.

HUMILITY AND WISDOM

John refers to himself in the third person on multiple occasions during some of the most critical events in the Gospel he penned.

> At the Last Supper: *"One of them, the disciple whom Jesus loved, was reclining next to him"* (John 13:23).
>
> At the Cross: *"When Jesus saw his mother there, and the disciple whom he loved standing nearby, he said to her, 'Woman, here is your son,' and to the disciple, 'Here is your mother.' From that time on, this disciple took her into his home"* (John 19:26-27).
>
> At the Empty Tomb: *"So she came running to Simon Peter and the other disciple, the one Jesus loved, and said, 'They have taken the Lord out of the tomb, and we don't know where they have put him!'"* (John 20:2).
>
> After the Resurrection: *"Then the disciple whom Jesus loved said to Peter, 'It is the Lord!'"* (John 21:7).
>
> After Peter's Reinstatement: *"Peter turned and saw that the disciple whom Jesus loved was following them. (This was the one who had leaned*

back against Jesus at the supper and had said, 'Lord, who is going to betray you?')" (John 21:20).

This son of Zebedee did this for one simple reason: to draw his reader's attention onto Jesus and away from himself. Unlike the other Gospels, where John receives plenty of ink, you will not find one instance of this son of Zebedee referring to himself by name. The only "Johns" he mentions by name are John the Baptist (John 1:19-34; 3:22-36; 4:1; 5:33-36; and 10:40-41), and Peter's father (1:42). By making himself low, John exalted his Savior and Teacher. He did not work to gain humility; it was "a natural by-product of spending time with Jesus."[27]

I'm sure you understand the implication. To honestly know Jesus' character and "stand tall" in the way that is consistent with who He created us to be, we have to start by looking up. Comparing ourselves to others does not make us wise; it certainly will not produce humility. Our education from our Master Teacher begins when we make ourselves low in light of His majestic height. And that is the posture where we remain until we breathe no more on this earth; especially if we want to develop depth of Christian wisdom, understand ourselves, and help others grow in their knowledge of Jesus.

Isaiah had that posture in his prophetic ministry: *"'Woe to me!' I cried. 'I am ruined! For I am a man of unclean lips, and I live among a people of unclean lips, and my eyes have seen the King, the LORD Almighty'"* (Isa. 6:5).

Paul had it in his apostolic leadership: *"For I am the least of the apostles and do not even deserve to be called an apostle, because I persecuted the church of God"* (1 Cor. 15:9). *"Although I am less than the least of all the Lord's people, this grace was given to me: to preach to the Gentiles the boundless riches of Christ"* (Eph. 3:8).

What makes the Scriptures come alive for me is the individuality of the writers "standing tall," given the height of our Lord. John was no exception. His lowly posture increased his significance, purpose, and wisdom; it did not diminish it. God works the same way in us also.

HUMILITY AND VANTAGE POINT

In my twenty years of preaching, I have yet to witness a Sunday morning where my congregation members dash to the front and center pew. Though it is the seat with the best vantage point, the cherry red cushions on those pews have always maintained their like-new condition. Perhaps this phenomenon exists because I am known to some as Reverend Fire Hydrant. The most likely explanation, however, is that people do not like to sit on the front row.

To sit close to a rabbi was an honor for their students in antiquity. Paul informs us that he was trained in the law of his fathers "under Gamaliel" (Acts 22:3). Such a description implies he sat at his feet. We see the idea more distinctly in Luke's Gospel, where Martha's sister Mary "sat at the Lord's feet listening to what he said" (Luke 10:39).

John informs us (as noted above) that he was "reclining" next to Jesus at the Last Supper (John 13:23). The Greek translates it as "he was reclining in the bosom of Jesus." John uses "bosom" just twice in his Gospel; the other instance is about Jesus being in the bosom of the Father (1:18).[28] While all the disciples had the honor of dining with our Lord, John had the closest vantage point.

Why does he give us this information? It would not be to suggest he ranked higher on the recipient list of Jesus' love than the others. If he did, John would not have excluded first-person references to himself from his Gospel. Instead, he uses the phrase to hint at the "tender regard" his Lord had for him.[29]

Jesus loved that John wanted to be as close to his Teacher, Friend, and Lord as humanly possible; John cherished being that close to Him just as much. He did not mind breaking in the cherry red pew cushion. In that sense, John may well be the Enoch of the New Testament. The latter lived to the ripe old age of 365 before God called him home (Gen. 5:23). Though John did not live that long, John "walked with God" (Gen. 5:24) just as faithfully as Enoch did.

John was close to his Maker, both literally and spiritually. Unlike the other disciples on this night, John could have heard His heartbeat. He might have even noticed the blood vessels of the Great I Am pulsating because of what Jesus knew was going to happen on Calvary the next day.

This son of Zebedee was not content with watching the parade or going inside to see the circus. He wanted to be a part of it. He was unsatisfied with watching his Master tame lions if he could not subdue them himself. Yes, friend, this disciple was uninterested in witnessing seas parting and suns standing still if he couldn't pray with the same type of faith that made those things possible.

Humility had produced activity in John: closeness to his Lord. And what he witnessed from that position, he recollects and communicates to us with a *sui generis* writing style. Matthew, Mark, and Luke are the Synoptic Gospels. The word *synoptic* comes from two Greek words: *syn* meaning "together" and *opsis*, meaning "view."[30] That is why you see similar stories and parables in them. But John's Gospel is different. It stands alone.

In the Synoptics, a request for a sign to believe usually receives Divine criticism (i.e., Matt. 12:38-39). John, however, has no trouble giving his audience "signs" (a.k.a. "miracles") as reasons to believe. Every time Jesus performed one, John makes sure to inform us of the significance of it:

1. Water to Wine – *"What Jesus did here in Cana of Galilee was the first of the signs through which he revealed his glory; and his disciples believed in him"* (John 2:11).

2. Healing of the Royal Official's Son in Capernaum – *"So he and all his household believed. This was the second sign Jesus performed after coming from Judea to Galilee"* (John 4:53b-54).

3. Healing of the Paralytic at Bethesda – *"The man went away and told the Jewish leaders that it was Jesus who had made him well"* (John 5:15).

4. Feeding of the Five Thousand – *"After the people saw the sign that Jesus performed, they began to say, 'Surely this is the Prophet who is to come into the world'"* (John 6:14).

5. <u>Walking on Water</u> – *"But he said to them, 'It is I; don't be afraid.' Then they were willing to take him into the boat, and immediately the boat reached the shore where they were heading"* (John 6:20-21).

6. <u>Healing of the Man Blind from Birth</u> – *"Then they turned again to the blind man, 'What have you to say about him? It was your eyes he opened'"* (John 9:17).

7. <u>Raising of Lazarus from the Dead</u> – *"Therefore many of the Jews who had come to visit Mary, and had seen what Jesus did, believed in him"* (John 11:45).

Only two of these miracles—the feeding of the five thousand and walking on water—appear in the Synoptic Gospels. The rest are exclusive to his Gospel. In His Divine wisdom, the God of Creation inspired John's hands to write about these other five because He wanted all of us to see an even grander scheme unfolding in the divulgement of Jesus' character than the already majestic one revealed in Matthew, Mark, and Luke. And God used the one disciple who sat in our Lord's bosom on that night to do it.

Also unique to John's Gospel is a series of statements by Jesus whereby He proclaims He is the Great I Am of the Old Testament. Together with the miracles above, they further elucidate the depth of Jesus' character:

1. *"'I am the bread of life. Whoever comes to me will never go hungry, and whoever believes in me will never be thirsty'"* (John 6:35).

2. *"'I am the light of the world. Whoever follows me will never walk in darkness, but will have the light of life'"* (John 8:12).

3. *"'I am the gate; whoever enters through me will be saved. They will come in and go out, and find pasture'"* (John 10:9).

4. *"'I am the good shepherd. The good shepherd lays down his life for the sheep'"* (John 10:11).

5. *"I am the resurrection and the life. The one who believes in me will live, even though they die; and whoever lives by believing in me will never die"* (John 11:25-26).

6. *"I am the way and the truth and the life. No one comes to the Father except through me"* (John 14:6).

7. *"I am the true vine, and my Father is the gardener"* (John 15:1).

Furthermore, when a detachment of Sanhedrin soldiers came to the Garden of Gethsemane to arrest Jesus, John tutors us with this observation: *"Jesus, knowing all that was going to happen to him, went out and asked them, 'Who is it you want?' 'Jesus of Nazareth,' they replied. 'I am he,' Jesus said. (And Judas the traitor was standing there with them.) When Jesus said, 'I am he,' they drew back and fell to the ground"* (John 18:4-6).

The last time those words were used in a statement, God uttered them to Moses through a bush He set on fire: *"Moses said to God, 'Suppose I go to the Israelites and say to them,* The God of your fathers has sent me to you, *and they ask me,* What is his name? *Then what shall I tell them?* God said to Moses, 'I AM WHO I AM. This is what you are to say to the Israelites: I AM has sent me to you'" (Exod. 3:13-14).

Jesus wanted the soldiers who arrested Him to know who He was: The Great I Am of the Old Testament! John wanted his readers to apperceive that as well. He knew that the bread from Heaven no longer fell out of the sky as manna in the wilderness. The Bread of Life was about to be handcuffed and taken to the Sanhedrin. Our Lord understood that the very Light that guided the Israelites to the Promised Land had just taught the soldiers what it means to be "enemies in your minds because of your evil behavior" (Col. 1:21) by just voicing Who He is.

John also cognized that the Good Shepherd was to head toward sure death at the hands of wolves "threatened by the voice of the paragon."[31] And he was well-qualified to teach his audience because he learned about his Master's virtue in the bosom of the God of the Exodus Himself. And the One who split the Red Sea loved that about John. Like David, he was *after* God's own heart in his life (1 Sam. 13:14).

Closeness to Jesus came in direct proportion to the degree John was willing to humble himself in light of his character. He welded them both together in his understanding of what being a disciple of Jesus entails. As a result, he gained the kind of spiritual wisdom that all of us who call Jesus "Lord" should strive to attain—the type that features depth of insight from personal experience and biblical knowledge and one that helps people grow in their understanding of Him.

HUMILITY AND COURAGE

A willingness to humble himself and follow his Lord, combined with time spent in the bosom of Jesus, produced courage in John. On the connection between the two, Ken Harrison observes, *"At the core of courage is humility . . . Courage isn't something conjured up at the moment that it is needed. It is the expression of your character at a moment of testing. Courage is the sum of all your virtues expressed at a single moment in time."*[32]

Our Lord's ministry to the masses did not stop and start with the five thousand He miraculously fed (Matt. 14:13-21) or the Sermon on the Plain (Luke 6:17-49). Luke tells us the Galileans who heard Jesus teach on the Sabbath were "amazed at his teaching, because his words had authority" (Luke 4:32).

By some scholastic indications, there were even more people present for the most influential sermon ever preached, the Sermon on the Mount, than any other proclamation event recorded in the New Testament.[33] God saved those who responded and believed by faith, and you will see them in Heaven.

But the masses did not serve Jesus at Calvary; neither did a lot of others. But John certainly did. In fact, on Good Friday, John showed his tremendous courage at a moment of intense testing. He did not abandon Jesus at the cross when it would have been much safer to do so. He stood tall and aced the exam.

In this beloved disciple's account of the Passion events, beginning with Jesus' arrest in Gethsemane (18:1), and concluding with His burial in Joseph of Arimathea's tomb (19:38-42), only three of the original Twelve play a pivotal role in the scene: Judas, who betrayed Jesus; Peter, who denied him; and John, who served our Lord when He needed it the most (19:25-27). John reintroduces other disciples in the story only after the resurrection: Thomas, when Jesus showed him proof of it (20:24-29); and several other disciples who were with Peter and John on the shores of the Sea of Galilee (21:2).

Think about that for a moment! In the most pivotal scene of John's Gospel from the standpoint of the sheer anguish our Lord had to face, this writing disciple thought best to mention two disciples who abandoned Jesus and one who ministered to Him. Peter didn't serve him. Nor did Andrew, James, Philip, Nathanael, Matthew, Thomas, Simon the Zealot, James the Lesser, or Judas, Not Iscariot. Only John served him on Calvary among his brethren. And such an act of service took considerable courage.

John is also modest about himself in his narration of the story. Instead of praising his faithfulness, John chooses to spotlight his Lord: *"Near the cross of Jesus stood his mother, his mother's sister, Mary the wife of Clopas, and Mary Magdalene. When Jesus saw his mother there, and the disciple whom he loved standing nearby, he said to her, 'Woman, here is your son,' and to the disciple, 'Here is your mother. From that time on, this disciple took her into his home"* (John 19:25-27).

This transference should have gone to James, the brother of Jesus. But he was nowhere to be found; neither were Jesus' brothers—Joseph, Simon, and Judas (Matt. 13:55). They all had forsaken him because they did not want to be tried and executed for treason. We do not know if any of the other disciples witnessed their bloody and bruised Rabbi hanging on a tree on this day. But we can glean from John's account that they did not have the same sightline as he did if they were present. He was the one out of Twelve standing nearby with the best vantage point.

John cared not about potential treason and insurrection charges; neither did these women. They knew from experience that being loved by God was an easy yoke and a light burden (Matt. 11:30). Consequently, they were willing to demonstrate the same servant-love Jesus showed them, especially John. He was a brother to Jesus Who was born for adversity (Prov. 17:17), one willing to love like Jesus, even if doing so meant arrest or death (John 15:13). Jesus modeled that on the cross; John modeled that to Jesus' mother in return. John was willing to serve the least of these at the moment: Mary, the mother of Jesus.

Walking away from the Great I Am to a perceivably safer position was not an option for this disciple whom Jesus loved. John loved his neighbor as much as he loved himself, even when it did not behoove him to do so. That neighbor just so happened to be God on the cross. For the time he spent with his Lord long before Christ's death provided the proper foundation for the courage he displayed. He knew the unconditional love of God toward him required reciprocation from him.

Only John among his brethren was spiritually alive at Calvary. No longer was he languishing in social snobbery and religious indignation. This son of Zebedee was now truly zoetic because his eyes were privileged to witness the One pierced for his transgressions and crushed for his iniquities (Isa. 53:5), fulfilling the Scriptures. That is life, and John had it. He stood tall without a word while the other disciples fellowshipped in spirit with King Saul at that moment, with their knees knocking and backs turned (1 Sam. 17:24). And such a courageous posture came courtesy of humility and fellowshipping with the Divine, right there in His bosom.

HUMILITY AND LOVE

Courage is not the only character that shines brightly from John's walk with Jesus; his genuine love for God and people radiates also. The love of God is the cornerstone of this beloved disciple's theological outlook. He refers to it forty-four times in his Gospel and thirty-seven times in 1 John.

Jesus loves because that's Who He is in His essence and character. Christ the Lord loved the world enough to sacrifice Himself (John 3:16); Mary, Martha, and Lazarus (John 11:5); and every disciple He called to Himself (John 13:14). Whether "red and yellow or black and white," anyone who has ever lived or ever will live is "precious in his sight" because Jesus loves everyone equally and completely.[34]

He loves preachers who shave their heads because they developed male pattern baldness at eighteen. He loves Democrats and Republicans. He loves sterling examples and failures. Regardless of race, creed, nationality, gender, or social standing, Jesus' love for humanity is all-encompassing because He is God. There are no variables or degrees to it either, even if you want to be more like Judas than you do Jesus. He still loves you.

But how John connects God's love to some of the more uncomfortable attributes of his character demonstrates a level of wisdom that he attained only through a meek and unpretentious walk with Jesus. He writes: "This is love: not that we loved God, but that he loved us and sent his Son as an atoning sacrifice for our sins" (1 John 4:10).

From John's theological lens, God's holiness and love are wed without the possibility of separation. Because God is holy, He will not tolerate sin. But instead of punishing me—which I most certainly deserve—God the Father initiated the love relationship I'm privileged to have with Him by punishing God the Son on Calvary. My Lord bore the wounds I inflicted upon Him and offered me "full and free" pardon.[35] That is the essence of the atonement our Triune God makes available to all who repent and believe.

Consequently, John does not want us to "pick up the ball of 'God is love' and run with it wherever we will."[36] He wants us to understand "God's love alongside his justice and wrath" instead.[37] If we separate these traits, Jesus becomes what we wish Him to be in our spiritual lives depending on our mood, whims, or circumstances. Binding them together, however, assures us of walking in the confidence that we do not have to initiate a relationship or restore it when we fail miserably. Jesus did both because He loves us. Calvary proves it. Our call is to draw near to Jesus (James 4:8) as John did.

THE BENEFIT OF HUMILITY AND CLOSENESS

I must confess that I often ask myself how a decision I make will benefit me. If I spend money on a new refrigerator, I hope to profit a colder Diet Coke. Purchasing a membership to Planet Fitness is not a charitable contribution for me; I plan to use it to get in shape. Though we may not reach all of our directional conclusions via the route of what we have to gain, weighing our resolutions by the degree of benefit is innate in each of us. Similarly, John benefited immensely from genuine humility and a close walk with Jesus. Walking with Jesus in this manner allowed John to "see" the Lord before some of the other disciples.

I love John 21 because it is the story of Peter taking fishing lessons, utterly oblivious to the One giving him instruction. John was not because he had spent considerable time in the lap of the Fisher of Men. After all, he knew Jesus is the Resurrection and the Life. Consequently, understanding the significance of the occasion, John nudged Peter and proclaimed: "It is the Lord!" (John 21:7).

Where the other disciples still saw only grief, John now had a triumphant perspective. What was still a shattered visage of faith for the others was now victory for this disciple. While they were still reeling from broken hopes and dreams, John had witnessed fulfillment. The crowds may have considered self-denial to be cumbersome, but John now beheld living in the love of the One Who loved him the most. Where the other disciples observed death, John's eyes forthwith gazed upon resurrection. John, after all, spotted Jesus, his resurrected Lord, while Peter and the others were back to doing what they did before they even met Him: fishing.

But, friend, that's not all this son of Zebedee saw. While exiled on the Isle of Patmos, John caught a glimpse of the future through an apocalyptic vision. He unveiled it in all its majesty and splendor in that book of the Bible we call Revelation because he had spent enough time in the lap of Jesus to recognize it as such.

Of importance to John's vision is "seven." The number of Divine completeness and perfection in biblical literature, it moves the narrative along. Addressing his prophecy to seven churches (Rev. 1:4) and with powerful imagery, John writes:

> I turned around to see the voice that was speaking to me. And when I turned I saw seven golden lampstands, and among the lampstands was someone like a son of man, dressed in a robe reaching down to his feet and with a golden sash around his chest . . . In his right hand he held seven stars, and coming out of his mouth was a sharp, double-edged sword. His face was like the sun shining in all its brilliance" (Rev. 1:12-13, 16).

What a vision! And it was just the beginning, too. He also saw seven seals, horns, eyes, angels, trumpets, thunders, heads, crowns, angels, plagues, bowls, mountains, and kings. John saw hope fulfilled, healing attained, longing rewarded, grace extended, hearts satisfied, love forever constant, and evil judged because he took the narrow road straight into the lap of Jesus and walked humbly with Him.

This disciple drew near to God and learned to live and exist in His life, love, and Spirit. As a result, God drew near to him and taught John: "'Not by might nor by power, but by my Spirit,' says the LORD Almighty" (Zech. 4:6). The same is possible for all of us if we will get up from the furthest seat from Him and march straight to the chair that is open right there at the lap of our resurrected Lord. Jesus loved that John wanted to sit there. And He loves it just as much when we do, too.

SOME QUESTIONS TO PONDER BEFORE MOVING ON

1. Read Psalm 145:18-19. In what ways can you draw near to God? What will He do in response, according to the text?

2. Read Luke 15. How might God orchestrate events in your life to show you that He is the Seeker in the parables and that He desires a relationship with you?

3. John's understanding of Jesus was directly related to his close fellowship with Him. How does our relationship with Jesus—or lack thereof—affect our knowledge of His character?

Chapter 5

THE ANDREW CALLING

PUT A BALL IN THE middle of two infants, and I will assure you they won't work out a plan to split playtime with it evenly. What they will do is utter "mine" at the same time! From birth, we all have a desire to put our best foot forward, even if that means stepping on others who happen to be in the way of where we want to go. We desire to be first—not last, or even second.

You remember all those playground pickup basketball games, don't you? You wanted to be one of the two who got to choose a team from among your peers. Don't lie. I did, too. When passed over for it, you raised your hand and yelled, "Pick me," like most everybody else. I had to do that because I was as uncoordinated as a one-legged man in a wire-balancing contest, and the odds of not being picked last significantly improved if I did.

I hated getting picked last. It hurt and stung, primarily because I had no trouble questioning my worth, considering my childhood environment. Getting selected last just confirmed what I already thought about myself: I was no good.

Ingrained within the very structure of our DNA lies an innate desire to be the sheriff, not the deputy. We usually want to be in charge. Unless, of course, you are a lot like Peter's brother in the New Testament. His name was Andrew.

He had a calling on his life, just like his brother: a mission God tailored to his unique skill sets and abilities. While Peter had a lot of flaws, shyness was not one of them. That's one of the reasons God called him to lead from the front. He also had no problem exercising his mandible, even if the words that spewed from it had no merit. Being the goat when he was wrong didn't bother Peter either because he wanted others to learn from his mistakes.

Andrew was his brother's polar opposite. You won't find foolish statements flowing from his lips. Never in a million years would he have remotely even considered mouthing comments sure to garner a Divine scolding from a cloud. He was smart enough to think *before* he opened his mouth. What a novel concept!

Andrew had no desire to be Peter. Even playground game-pickers in those days would have had a hard time picking him. He was the lad who didn't raise his hand, though he wanted to play.

FAITHFUL BEHIND THE SCENES

After teaching them a parable about workers in a vineyard, Jesus voiced these words to His disciples: "So the last will be first, and the first will be last" (Matt. 20:16).

Andrew took this dictum literally. Though not in the spotlight, he desired to be faithful in the simple things often not noticed or applauded by the masses. But they are equally important in Jesus' kingdom economy.

If any disciple fit the description of being comfortable behind the scenes, Andrew did. He's referenced only thirteen times in the entire New Testament. Want to take a wild stab at how many times his brother gets holy ink? If you guessed 158, you would be right. Call me if you did because I need some investment advice!

Andrew owns no spiritual copyright to any book in the New Testament. On the other hand, his brother owns three: 1 Peter, 2 Peter, and a Gospel penned by one of his protégés named Mark. Irenaeus of Lyons, the second century bishop of the church in Smyrna, was the first early church father to tell us about the connection between Peter and the Gospel of Mark. He states:

"Mark, the disciple and interpreter of Peter, did also hand down to us in writing what had been preached by Peter."[38]

In today's ministry world, Peter would have inked a major Christian publishing deal and embarked on an international book tour. Andrew, on the other hand, would have driven him to the airport before heading to church to teach a small group. From God's perspective, though, both of their ministries were equally important. Because without high character and honest Andrews leading by example behind the scenes, no Peters or Johns can guide from the front.

SUBMISSIVE AND WITHOUT VAINGLORY

Andrew had no desire to attain fame or acclaim for following Jesus. He served his Providential audience gladly; he probably even kept his brother in line. Not only did Andrew support the mission of Jesus behind the scenes, but he also felt comfortable enough in his skin to accept his often-overlooked and undervalued post. See if you catch my draft by these examples:

1. "As Jesus was walking beside the Sea of Galilee, he saw two brothers, Simon called Peter <u>and his brother Andrew</u>" (Matt. 4:18—emphasis mine).

2. "These are the names of the twelve apostles: <u>first</u>, Simon (who is called Peter) and <u>his brother Andrew</u>" (Matt. 10:2—emphasis mine).

3. "As Jesus walked beside the Sea of Galilee, he saw Simon <u>and his brother Andrew</u> casting a net into the lake, for they were fisherman" (Mark 1:16—emphasis mine).

4. "When morning came, he called his disciples to him and chose twelve of them, whom he also designated apostles: Simon (whom he named Peter), <u>his brother Andrew</u>" (Luke 6:13-14—emphasis mine).

5. "Andrew, <u>Simon Peter's brother</u>, was one of the two who heard what John had said and who had followed Jesus" (John 1:40—emphasis mine).

6. "Another of his disciples, Andrew, <u>Simon Peter's brother</u>, spoke up" (John 6:8—emphasis mine).

That's right, my friend. On six of the thirteen occasions, Andrew gets divinely inspired New Testament ink; he's referred to in a way that seems to make him inferior to his brother, at least on the surface. Bummer! How would you have felt if you walked in his shoes?

I have an older brother. Throughout my childhood, folks reminded me of it. That bothered me. Similar statements about Andrew could have disconcerted him. But they didn't. You see, every time Andrew heard his seemingly inferior introduction—most especially when Jesus first called him from the shores of the Sea of Galilee—he had one of two choices to make.

First, he could plead his case that he ought to be first by trying to persuade his Divine Caller that he was just as talented and capable as his brother. Richard the Lionheart's brother, John, would have certainly done this if he were Andrew. In the early part of the twelfth century, Richard was put in prison in Austria as he returned to England from the Holy Land after the Third Crusade. His brother seized the throne while he was gone because he wanted to be *King* John, not John, King Richard I of England's Little Brother.[39]

Secondly, he could accept his role and call other people to join him. Lillian Disney did that, and your kids and mine are all the better for it. Had Walt Disney had his way, the mouse you know as Mickey would have been Mortimer.

Also doubling as his secretary, Lillian rejected that anathema of a name as soon as she heard it and pitched the famous appellation to him instead. Without Lillian's leadership behind the scenes, the mouse that is Mickey has no voice to welcome parents from all over the world as they descend upon Orlando, Florida, to watch their kids smile while they pay a hundred grand for an unlimited-refill fountain drink. Mortimer does.[40] Andrew thankfully chose the latter. He submitted first to the Lord's authority and then to his brother's. That would have been as difficult for him to stomach as it would have been for me. But without that submission, the work of Jesus cannot go forward in the world. And just as important, if this essential component of Christian maturity gets cast by the wayside, the Gospel work of the church will get hijacked by inwardly hostile and rebellious individuals like John, the brother of Richard I, and Judas Iscariot. I've seen it happen.

The moment Andrew rejected vainglory to follow Jesus, he embraced submission and all that it entails. Sometimes that word carries a negative connotation because some people use it to put down other people. It is, however, paramount for organizational relationships to prosper, most especially Christian ones.

For example, how many times have you seen this scenario play out in church? The pastor or group leader prays about a direction. When the direction comes and the leader presents the vision to the group, someone raises his hand in the back, stands up, and says, "I have a better idea!" While his idea might be better, the moment he stands and calls people to follow him, instead of those whom God has commissioned to do the leading, is the moment the group becomes divided in mission and purpose. If the leader is wise, he will listen to the person who desires to be first and incorporate some of his good ideas into the plan. But if he allows the Absalom to lead the group in that situation, the church's mission cannot advance. It can only splinter. On the other hand, leaders with integrity behind the scenes can impact public ones positively, particularly under the covering of love.

I wish I could have been privy to Andrew's conversations with his spotlight sibling after he stuck his foot in his mouth. I'm sure they would have been humorous: "Hey brother, you shouldn't have opened your trap about constructing tabernacles as God spoke from a cloud. That made about as much sense as tight slacks." To which Peter would have probably responded: "Tell me something I don't know. I'm still first, though. So, know your role, brother!"

Without putting Christ first in their lives, those conversations could not have taken place. Destructive sibling rivalry would have prevailed. Consequently, the brothers—and eventually the rest of the group—would have splintered from infighting because of a desire to be first. They didn't, though, because submission and rejecting vainglory were the keys that drove their mission bus. And people's lives were changed because they did—including yours and mine.

BENEFITED FROM LISTENING INSTEAD OF TALKING

I used to watch Superman when I was a youngster. He never made a dime by saving the world from the likes of Lex Luthor, Solomon Grundy, or Kryptonite Man.[41] Much like the caped hero in his world, Andrew's preference for being out of the spotlight and his knack for doing more listening and less talking made him keenly aware of the significance of the mission and message of Jesus before the others in his world.

Contrary to Jimmy Olsen, Perry White, and the rest of the higher-ups at *The Daily Planet*, Superman never wanted to make the headlines for confronting the problems of the world for the benefit of humanity. Andrew didn't either. Both valued the mission above the accolades that often come with a successful undertaking.

The spotlight leaders—Peter, James, and John—are sometimes grouped together in the Gospels. On one of those occasions, the scene just after Jesus' transfiguration, a fight breaks out among them just after they witnessed Divine majesty on the mountain. Instead of glowing within by humbling themselves on the way down, they decide to banter back and forth the next day about who was going to be the greatest among them. As a result, Jesus rebuked them sharply, saying, "For it is the one who is least among you all who is the greatest" (Luke 9:48).

In contrast, in the only biblical passage in the New Testament where Andrew plays a major role, he teams up with Philip—not with his brother or the Zebedee siblings—and says absolutely nothing to anyone, except Jesus: "Now there were some Greeks among those who went up to worship at the festival. They came to Philip, who was from Bethsaida in Galilee, with a request. 'Sir,' they said, 'we would like to see Jesus.' Philip went to tell Andrew; Andrew and Philip in turn told Jesus" (John 12:20-22). Andrew had no time to engage in chest-beating banter like his brother. He was too perceptive and wise for that. He was more keenly aware of the mission than those too busy trying to outrank each other. That's probably one reason John saw fit to insert this into the narrative of his Gospel.

Followers of Jesus with an "Andrew Calling" do what the Lord wants them to do—no more and no less. They want to serve and love. You will not find an Andrew in today's world scratching the proverbial back of someone to get something in return, nor will you see them performing a good deed to get lauded with praise. Those things mean nothing to people like Andrew. They scratch the proverbial backs of others without the expectation of a favorable return. They know long before they stretch out their fingers that they serve others as unto the Lord (Matt. 25:40). Spotlight leaders often have a problem with that concept. Not Andrews. They glory in it.

VALUED WHAT OTHERS OVERLOOKED

I've thrown away scores of empty juice boxes in my lifetime. They have no value to me, so I proudly relegate them to the trash heap. But not to the geniuses who figured out a way to make purses out of them and convince retail chains to sell them to folks like my wife. They saw waste and turned it into something of value and worth.

Of all his traits, this one truly made Andrew great: he saw value in what most others overlook. His spiritual lenses were certainly not foggy in this famous scene: "Another of his disciples, Andrew, Simon Peter's brother, spoke up, 'Here is a boy with five small barley loaves and two small fish, but how far will they go among so many?'" (John 6:8-9). Andrew's faith isn't perfect here. He doubts Jesus can turn these into enough food to feed five thousand people. But without a mustard seed of faith, he would have never had the courage to speak up, especially given his propensity to tame his tongue! He saw value in what the rest of the group overlooked. Do you see hope in hopeless situations? Are you willing to scour the trash heap for pearls like Andrew did? It takes great faith to do that, even if it isn't perfect.

Speaking of faith, did you notice *when* Andrew and Philip took the Greeks to see Jesus? It was during a feast. It wasn't just any feast either; it was the Feast of Tabernacles. The special occasion commemorated Israel's exodus from Egypt, the greatest act of salvation and redemption in the Old Testament. Occurring on Tishri 15-22, the feast was both a harvest festival and a commemoration of the event. Booths, or *sukkahs,* were temporary dwellings farmers lived in during harvest time. Israel also resided in these "tabernacles" during their forty years of travel in the desert after their exodus from Egypt. So to keep this event alive in their theological memories, Jews sojourned to Jerusalem to construct and sleep in them.

A couple important Old Testament events occurred during the festival: Solomon dedicated the first temple during it (1 Kings 8:2), and Ezra proclaimed the Word of God to post-exilic Israel (Neh. 8:13-17).

Dancing, singing, and chanting during a procession of lights were a big part of the festivities. Unfortunately, Israel's understanding of the whole event was flawed. They didn't see the connection between a festival of lights and their mission to be a light to others. They should have because light denotes the ability to see. To prance around Jerusalem with candelabras while oblivious to the needs of others wasn't God's intent for them. God designed Israel as a city on a hill not easily hidden (Matt. 5:14), not as a dark cavern.

Philip and Andrew were different. They glowed with the character of the Almighty the moment they introduced the pagans to Jesus. Such an action does not seem like a big deal in our world; it was in both of theirs, though. You see, at this point in the story, the spotlight disciples were unaware God had a plan to graft the Gentiles into His redemptive purposes by faith alone (Eph. 3:1-13). These out-of-the-spotlight leaders didn't make the same mistake.

They knew that Jesus' words offered spiritual life to the Jew *and* the Gentile. That is why they introduced them to Jesus *during* the salvific festival. They knew the Greeks needed a Savior just like they did because they spent less time talking and more time listening to the One Who dwelt among them (John 1:14). Where the other disciples saw pure trash, Philip and Andrew saw beautiful treasures waiting to be found and claimed.

My friend, caring and helping people who can do absolutely nothing for you is the hallmark of sincere faith. We also love people, regardless of whether they believe and think like we do because Jesus is Love. And the best way to demonstrate our fondness of our merciful Savior is to introduce prospective Christ-followers to Him when the opportunity knocks at our mission door, just like Andrew and Philip did. And to do that, we have to be approachable like they were. Such an ethic is right for us, and will always be, and correct for church leaders, and always will be until Christ comes again. When we do something for "the least of these" (Matt. 25:40), we are modeling the very ethos of God in our world, just as Philip and Andrew did in theirs.

THE EXAMPLE

We pass by the homeless every day while we are driving. When we see them while idling at a red light, we often come up with every type of excuse we can cognitively produce to justify not helping them:

"He just wants money to drink."

"She makes a good living doing this."

Instead of offering up a litany of "Derrick excuses," Andrew would stop right in the street in heavy traffic and say, "Would you like something to eat?" He would see value in what I'm often guilty of overlooking. He might even invite them to a worship service at his church and reserve a valued place for them. James tells us, "If you show special attention to the man wearing fine clothes and say, 'Here's a good seat for you,' but say to the poor man,

'You stand there' or 'Sit on the floor by my feet,' have you not discriminated among yourselves?" (James 2:3-4).

Jesus walked the highways, streets, and back alleys seeking out those who needed His love. He recruited and pardoned a motley crew of rebels with different skill sets and turned them into a ministry-functioning team to show it to others. It was a faith plan evidenced through active mercy and service. That was God's plan for the world then; it is still His plan for it now. And it takes not just the Peters, James, and Johns of the Kingdom of God to do that. It also requires the Andrews.

SOME QUESTIONS TO PONDER BEFORE MOVING ON

1. Read Luke 22:26-27. How does God judge greatness in His Kingdom economy? In what ways do you genuinely serve others without expecting anything in return?

2. Read 3 John 9-12. List Diotrephes' character attributes. How might such a personality become dangerous in a spiritual setting?

3. Like Andrew, Demetrius is a lesser-known hero of the New Testament. Why? In what ways can you model the attitudes of Demetrius and Andrew in your life?

Chapter 6
FINDING PHILIP

HE HAS BEEN ONE OF my best friends for over twenty years. Because of that friendship with Jay, people who knew us in college usually go into uncontrollable fits of hyperventilation when they find out both of us are in ministry today. To them, we were the Trouble Twins. Whenever problems occurred that are synonymous with the words *prank* and *mischief* at the private Christian institution we attended, we were blamed and accursed.

We were accused so much for things we did *not* do that we came to revel in and take credit for things we *should* have done or *would* have done had we thought about it. We covered all four walls of our dorm room in write-ups from the school's administration and entitled the whole display The Walls of Shame.

Grace was not a word in the administration's vocabulary with us—and for perfectly good reasons. Thankfully, though, it was in the lexicon of a campus policeman on one cold winter night. We were out doing something rather doltish like shooting firecrackers at the girl's dorm or removing the wheels from the school president's car. You know, innocent things like that.

What we were doing on this night I cannot remember. But I do recall hearing a siren and running into the woods. Had we split up in our escape plan, we would have never gotten caught. But because the words *Jay, sneak, quiet,* and *leaf* do not belong in the same sentence, we got busted. When

Sherlock Holmes, Jr. seized us, he pointed the flashlight directly into our eyes and quipped, "Why am I not surprised it's Derrick and Jay?"

We warranted more Walls of Shame decorations from him on that night. Our actions even merited the sentence of "breaking rocks in the hot sun" the next day because we "fought the law and the law won."[42] Each of us got a pair of gloves and a towel instead. More importantly, instead of sentencing us to the rock quarry, Sherlock just said, "You guys can't afford any more administrative write-ups without getting kicked out of this joint. This one is on me. I'll take you guys back to the dorm."

Grace sought and caught us. It covered us, cleaned us, and led us safely home. We deserved the administration's wrath; we got unmerited favor instead. From that point on, our pranks ceased. We didn't exactly become the type of folks that could run uncontested for school president. But neither did we get any more letters from the administration with the title *Violation 368*.

There were some disciples, like John and James, who immediately left their boat and followed Jesus when He called them. But unlike Jay and me in the woods that night, some were better at hiding from Him. All that means in the economy of an omnibenevolent God is that He would have to go to greater lengths to seek, find, love, cover, and clean them. Philip is such an example. He didn't pursue Jesus; the Lord ransacked the world looking for him instead. He spent a great deal of energy doing it, too, because Philip was hard to find.

GOD THE SEEKER

Matthew, Mark, and Luke refer to this disciple only by name and just in association with the other eleven disciples. Don't confuse him with the Philip who led the Ethiopian Eunuch to Christ either. He was one of seven chosen to serve as a deacon in the first Christian church ever, located in Jerusalem (Acts 6:5).

Only John inserts him into the narrative of his Gospel; what we know about Philip comes, therefore, via his ink and quill. And the Beloved Disciple limits him there to just four scenes: his calling (1:43-48); the feeding of the five thousand (6:5-7); the witness to the Greeks at the Feast of Tabernacles (12:20-22); and Jesus' claim to exclusivity (14:8-9). Philip, however, plays an active and integral narrative role in all four.

But before John tells us anything about who he was or where he was from, he chooses first to read us in on God's character: "The next day Jesus decided to leave for Galilee. <u>Finding Philip</u>, he said to him, 'Follow me'" (John 1:43—emphasis mine).

In the language of the New Testament, the participle *finding* denotes the action of Jesus continually searching until He found and obtained what He sought. Like a treasure hunter sifting through sand in a quest to find something of worth, Jesus combed for Philip until He unearthed him because He thought he was worth the effort.

Jesus was the initial Seeker in Philip's story. John makes sure we know it, too. What follows next is a comment from John about where he was from: "Philip, like Andrew and Peter, was from the town of Bethsaida" (John 1:44).

This town, where Jesus fed the multitudes with five loaves of bread and two fishes, was one of two cities that became the object of His holy wrath for rejecting Him later in His ministry: "Woe to you, Chorazin! Woe to you, Bethsaida! For if the miracles that were performed in you had been performed in Tyre and Sidon, they would have repented long ago in sackcloth and ashes. But I tell you, it will be more bearable for Tyre and Sidon on the day of judgment than for you" (Matt. 11:21-22).

Jesus was right. In the first Jewish War (66-70 CE), the historian Flavius Josephus was himself responsible for Bethsaida's defense against the Romans. Unfortunately, he fell from his horse in the battle and helplessly watched as centurions reduced the city to rubble.[43] And gravel it remained for over two thousand years until a group of archaeologists sifted through it and found the city's gate.⁴⁴

Had Jesus not found Philip inside Bethsaida before this tragic moment, he might have suffered the same fate as the rest of her inhabitants. He wasn't in the debris, though; Jesus found him and brought him out of that town of impending doom long before her final moments.

Philip was not the only disciple Jesus searched for either. Tax collectors and sinners like Matthew once invited Jesus to a meal. He accepted. But the Pharisees and teachers saw Jesus eating with them and muttered, "This man welcomes sinners and eats with them" (Luke 15:2).

Jesus tells them why in a series of three parables:

Suppose a shepherd has a hundred sheep and loses one. Does he not leave the ninety-nine to look for the one? Then, when he finds it, he puts it on his shoulders, rushes home, and then throws a party because he found him. Do you search for sinners who need my Father as I do, preacher boys?

Or how about a woman who loses one silver coin out of ten? Will she not turn over everything in the house to find it? When she does, she rejoices and dances until her feet are sore. Should I not look for folks in desperate need of a gracious encounter with the Divine like that? How would not conducting this type of search and rescue endeavor be consistent with My character?

Better yet, how about a prodigal son who returns home with his head hung from the shame of squandering his inherited wealth on wild living? He didn't even have the time to say "please forgive me, father" because his merciful dad had already done that long before. The prodigal could only accept his welcome.

Do you see God through that lens, guys? I know you're clergy and all; but if you don't see Him for what He is—the Seeker and Savior of sinners—then you've never met Him, nor do you know anything about Him. That's because in the Bible—yes, the one that My Father inspired from His eternal abode—God Himself is the Seeker.

PHILIP THE SEEKER

Philip had been caught and arrested by that "reckless and raging fury" that is the love of God.[45] Then he became a seeker of men himself. John tells us, "Philip <u>found</u> Nathanael and told him, 'We have <u>found</u> the one Moses wrote about in the Law, and about whom the prophets also wrote—Jesus of Nazareth, the son of Joseph.' 'Nazareth! Can anything good come from there?' Nathanael asked. 'Come and see,' said Philip" (John 1:45-46—emphasis mine).

John uses the same verb stem to describe Philip's actions as he did for the actions of Jesus. The Lord found Philip after continually searching for him; Philip, in turn, scoured Galilee for Nathanael until he sighted him. Only a disciple of the Lord Jesus can make another one.[46] And Philip's spiritual reduplication was directly related to the Divine company he kept at that moment.

Albert Schweitzer once famously quipped, "There are only three ways to teach a child. The first is by example, the second is by example, and the third is by example."[47]

Jesus modeled that by seeking Philip, who then facsimiled the same behavior. We must repeat the process because discipleship happens by being God's people in the world as we go about our business every day. We don't have to go overseas to be great in the economy of His Kingdom, though we indeed should if He calls us to. We only have to love those around us—especially within our sphere of influence—with the love of Christ, no more or less.

Though an example, Philip had his share of flaws. One of his biggest foibles concerned his spiritual thinking. He mistakenly thought they "found" the predicted Prophet, Who was more significant than Moses (Deut. 18:15). No one *naturally* seeks after God to find Him because He's not lost. We are.

David agrees: "The Lord looks down from heaven on all mankind to see if there are any who understand, any who <u>seek God</u>. All have turned away, all have become corrupt; there is no one who does good, not even one" (Psalm 14:2-3).

So does Paul: "As it is written: 'There is no one righteous, not even one; there is no one who understands; there is <u>no one who seeks God</u>" (Rom. 3:10-12—emphasis mine).

Oh, and don't forget Jesus: "<u>No one</u> can come to me unless the Father who sent me draws them, and I will raise them up at the last day. It is written in the Prophets: 'They will all be taught by God'" (John 6:44-45—emphasis mine).

When the "Hound of Heaven"[48] first found Philip, He gave him the capacity to emulate His character to Nathanael—but not before. Israel, as the Lord's chosen vineyard, had that latitude in the Old Testament but chose disobedience instead (Jer. 29:11-19). We must not. Philip would agree.

AN ALMOST METAMORPHOSIS

Oh, how small our concept of the Gospel is when we think God became flesh and dwelt among us only to save us and give us an afterlife bus ride to a pie in the sky by and by! It was also designed by God to produce metamorphosis within us in the here and now. That big word in the last sentence means a "change of physical form, structure, or substance, <u>especially</u> by supernatural means."[49]

That's precisely Jesus' aim in His next dialogue with Philip:

> The Jewish Passover Festival was near. When Jesus looked up and saw a great crowd coming toward him, he <u>said to Philip</u>, "Where shall we buy bread for these people to eat?" He asked this only to test him, for he already had in mind what he was going to do. Philip answered him, "It would take more than half a year's wages to buy enough bread for each one to have a bite" (John 6:4-7—emphasis mine).

Our Savior wasn't finished with Philip when He found him. That was only the beginning. Here, the Lord led Philip's growth process by tailoring a curriculum at his "School of Strengthening Weaknesses" specifically for him. It was only one question: one designed to test his faith. His answer revealed both his personality strengths and weaknesses.

Philip's strength was his mental capacity to understand the bottom line and what was right in front of him. I would make a beeline to Bethsaida and hire him as my accountant were he alive today. His weakness was his propensity to resort to hopelessness and despair when the numbers didn't blackline. Finding solutions to real problems wasn't an instinct Philip had mastered; he was an expert in finding irregularities that could cripple the mission, though.

Had Jesus asked him to walk on water, Philip would have probably replied, "It is physically and scientifically impossible to walk on water, Lord. Therefore, I am not willing to get out of the boat, even though I'm well aware that the Lord Who made the lake is calling me to." Jesus, however, gave him the test because He wanted him to learn, like Peter, to say, "Tell me to walk on water, Lord, and I'll do it."

Philip's strengths were needed, and Jesus placed him among the Twelve to be effective. But while using him in his competencies, Jesus also exposed his weaknesses to increase his faith. That is how biblical faith works. It wouldn't be faith otherwise.

Unless Philip got to the point where he could believe by faith that turning a couple of fish and loaves of bread was all in a day's work for the Master Who called him, he would be hopelessly frustrated at trying to put new wine into old wineskins. Jesus knew that. He knew that instead of trusting in what he could see, Philip needed to believe Him for what he couldn't do or solve by himself. And Jesus asked that question because He's the Disciple-seeker, not just the Soul-finder.

DOUBT REMAINED

I must remind my children of many things. Cleaning their rooms ranks number one on my list. Emphasizing to them that I clothe my discipline in love comes in a close second. The challenge with raising kids is to get them to believe that doing what they don't want or like to do is for their benefit and development. Faith works the same way.

Even after personally witnessing the miracle of the feeding of the five thousand, Philip still had trouble believing Jesus because his brain was hardwired to trust just in the bottom line. In another narrative scene, John tells us: "Philip said, 'Lord, show us the Father and that will be enough for us.' Jesus answered: 'Don't you know me, Philip, even after I have been among you such a long time? Anyone who has seen me has seen the Father. How can you say, 'Show us the Father?' 'Don't you believe that I am in the Father, and that the Father is in me?'" (John 14:8-10).

After Jesus claimed exclusivity and to be the only way to the Father (John 14:6), Philip wanted assurance via a theophany, a visual manifestation of God the Father Himself. Though God is invisible, the Bible contains a host of scenes where He made Himself visible to His chosen vessels.

God appeared to Abraham via theophany on three different occasions (Gen. 15:1; 17:1; and 18:1). Moses' burning bush experience is arguably the most famous one (Ex. 19). After King Uzziah died, Isaiah "saw the Lord, high and exalted, seated on a throne; and the train of his robe filled the temple" (Isa. 6:1). So, to seize the moment under the influence of the Petrine Impulse, Philip asked Jesus to include the Twelve among the recipients of Divine theophany.

He didn't expect the gentle chastisement that followed. Jesus couched it in the form of three questions related to His Divinity. Three is the number of completeness in the Bible. Consequently, the way Jesus rebuked Philip was no mistake. It denoted that Jesus' testimony about Himself—which the disciples had observed through miracles and heard through His "I Am" statements—was complete. Furthermore, it should have been enough for all of them to conclude He was Divine, including Philip.

Had they paid attention in Jesus' Sermon on the Mount, the disciples wouldn't have been asked by Jesus the first question because they would have already known the answer. The same is true for the second inquiry. The third centered around Philip's lack of belief, faith, and trust in Christ

Himself. He'd already had that exam and didn't do so well. Now he does even worse on the retake.

Don't throw stones at Philip, though. He's just like you and me, isn't he? Regardless of how long we have walked with Jesus, we always seem to struggle with doubting Him on some level. My doubts are different than Philip's were; but both types question God's sufficiency and character, a spiritual malady birthed and voiced first by the serpent in Eden. And if I don't trust God through them, that's where I remain—as do you.

PHILIP'S SIGNIFICANCE

Philip's story is remarkable because it has less to do with him and more to do with the nature of God and how He works in the world. He's the Seeker. Period. He seeks a relationship with us and loves us enough to remind us that we can trust Him. He will even resort to Divine discipline if He must because He loves us that much.

This disciple lived in a world much different than ours. While ours is individualistic, Philip's was one in which people judged others by whether they brought honor or shame to their family, community, country, and faith. Philip would have never welcomed back a prodigal family member into the fold who brought shame to all of these. He would have shunned that person instead and considered it honorable to do so.

Jesus is so much different, though. He seeks sinners. "But while he was still a long way off, his father saw him and was filled with compassion for him; he ran to his son, threw his arms around him and kissed him" (Luke 15:20).

Patriarchs in Philip's world didn't run to greet someone, especially a wasteful son like this one. Such an action would have been shameful for the father to do because he had to pull his cloak up, thereby exposing his legs. But the father in this parable didn't care. The moment this father saw him—which implies, by the way, that he was always looking—he ran to him and took his boy's shame upon himself.

Similarly, Jesus took our shame upon Himself so that we can become righteous in His eyes (2 Cor. 5:21). He did that for the prodigal son, for Philip, for you, and for me because God is the Seeker. You don't find Him. He comes after you with a passionate fury and won't quit the chase until He gets His hands on what He's after: you!

SOME QUESTIONS TO PONDER BEFORE MOVING ON

1. Read Psalm 119:176. How has God sought you out and gained your attention when you have gone astray?

2. Read Jonah 1. How did God seek Jonah when he went astray? What happens when we run from what God calls us to do? What are you called to do?

3. Read Psalm 119:9-16. List some ways you can seek after God in your life right now.

Chapter 7

NATHANAEL: WITHOUT GUILE, BUT FULL OF PREJUDICE

I KNOW YOU'VE ENGAGED IN a conversation like this while out on the town with your sweetie:

"Where shall we eat, dear?"

"Doesn't matter."

"Okay. What about Olive Garden?"

"No. I'm not in the mood for Italian."

"Bummer. Then what about Chipotle?"

"Who is that? Is he a friend of yours?"

"No. That's a restaurant, boss lady. What about Panera Bread? I know you like that place."

"No. I went there for lunch with my girlfriends, so we could sit and gossip about people."

"Pizza then?"

"Not really in the mood for it."

"Then where?"

"Doesn't matter."

When I get in those conversations with my better half, I cut that back and forth jibber jab off expeditiously by proclaiming what no wife wants to hear about fine dining:

"Okay. I'll surprise you."

She frowns immediately because she knows from experience that in my lexicon the word *surprise* means the Waffle House. I love that dive because I can inform the waitress there that I want my hash browns scattered, smothered, and covered, and she will know exactly what I mean. On the other hand, my wife loathes it because she cannot find anything decently comestible to suit her.

There is a disciple known for one of the most famous slogans in the entire Bible. When his friend Philip asked him to jump on Galilee Street and head north on Jezreel Valley Avenue en route to that no-traffic-light town called Nazareth—a Galilean city not referenced in the Old Testament—to see the Messiah, he responded, "Nazareth! Can anything good come from there?" (John 1:46).

John calls this disciple Nathanael on six occasions, five of which occur in the first chapter of his Gospel. You'll be frustrated trying to identify him in the Synoptic Gospels, though, because they don't even mention a Nathanael. But they do recognize a Bartholomew. You don't have to be a biblical studies savant to conclude they are the same individual either. On all but one occasion, they put him just after Philip on their lists of disciples.

John reserves that place for Nathanael, not on a list—because he doesn't have one—but within the context of the one major narrative scene where he plays a part. And what he tells us about him should challenge us to think before we decide to judge others, especially God Himself.

THE ORIGINS OF GUILELESSNESS AND PREJUDICE

Nathanael's penchant for prejudice began very early in his life, perhaps even in his mother's womb. They chose to name him *Nathanael*, meaning "God has given." It's constructed from two Hebrew words: *El* (God) and *Natan* (to give).[50]

Both of these words occur in the same sentence over one hundred times in the Old Testament, thirty-eight of which occur in the most influential historical book: Deuteronomy. Structured as five sermons Moses delivered on the Plains of Moab to the second generation of Israelites, Deuteronomy has three central themes: (1) receipt of the land God promised Abraham; (2) blessings for obedience; and (3) curses for disobedience, including banishment.

Nathanael's parents grew up hearing rabbis quote beautiful verses relating to these substantive subject matters, like: "Now, Israel, hear the decrees and laws I am about to teach you. Follow them so that you may live and may go in and take possession of the land that the Lord, the God of your ancestors, is giving you" (Deut. 4:1). "But you will cross the Jordan and settle in the land the Lord your God is giving you as an inheritance, and he will give you rest from all your enemies around you so that you will live in safety" (Deut. 12:10).

They both knew that names meant something in Hebrew culture. And labeling their son Nathanael was a way of demonstrating their faith in the God of Israel: the one true and living God Who gives and keeps His promises. Mr. and Mrs. Tolmai wanted their son and those who would encounter him to know that.

You read that right. Nathanael's dad was Tolmai. Nathanael's surname is Bartholomew, meaning "son of Tolmai." It's also important for understanding his story because the designated marker "son of" was usually reserved for the male progeny of an individual who was very well-known and respected in the world of the Bible.

We've already seen this with John and James, the sons of Zebedee (Matt. 4:21-22). But if you search the Old Testament, you'll find a cornucopia of examples. The framer of 1 and 2 Samuel assigned David as "the son of an Ephrathite named Jesse" just before he used five stones and a slingshot to route Goliath (1 Sam. 17:12). Similarly, the framer of 1 and 2 Chronicles deemed Solomon "the son of David" before describing how great the Lord made him (2 Chron. 1:1). And let us never forget how Mark introduced us to the most famous son in the history of the world: "The beginning of the gospel about <u>Jesus Christ, the son of God</u>" (Mark 1:1—emphasis mine).

While Bartholomew's dad wasn't in the biblical fame stratosphere of Jesus, he was someone known to others in and around the Galilean city of Cana (John 21:2). Cana was the locale where Jesus demonstrated that His water-to-wine recipe tasted Divine (John 2:1-11) and where His healing powers traveled through thin air to heal a royal official's son in Capernaum (John 4:46-54). And Tolmai was a somebody there; his son, Mr. Nathanael Bartholomew, was living proof of it. People in Cana knew "natan el bar tolmai" meant "God had given a Tolmai a son."

Nathanael took the theological implications of his name seriously. He was honest and sincere; he was without guile. When Jesus called him, He even said as much: "Here truly is an Israelite in whom there is no deceit" (John 1:47).

But as honest and sincere as he was, Nathanael was also proud of himself for being so. That's why he threw Nazareth under the bus when Philip told him the Messiah was there. If you combine deep, personal prejudice with the ability to give those demons a voice through theological rhetoric, you have a recipe for the makings of real evil in the name of God. History is replete with examples too numerous to list.

But when Jesus encountered Nathanael and called him by grace through faith alone, this son of Tolmai was quick to reverse himself and deal with his prejudgments of God and people. As a result, he learned to see the mission of Jesus through the eyes of Christ Himself. And it all started when he decided to go inside the discipleship tent to be Jesus' pupil.

HONEST, SINCERE, AND FAITHFUL

Nathanael practiced his faith honestly and sincerely. John tells us in his Gospel that Jesus saw him under a fig tree before their encounter (John 1:48). Israel had one temple but thousands of fig trees in antiquity. He went to the temple to worship like everyone else. But Nathanael took the time to do something a lot of Israelites didn't think about as much: he practiced the presence of God outside the temple. This guileless disciple wasn't under a fig tree taking a nap. He was worshipping God personally.

These trees are synonymous with the blessings of God in biblical literature. Adam and Eve sewed fig leaves to cover themselves after they sinned against Him (Gen. 3:7). The blessings of inheriting the Promised Land meant that God gave Israel "a land with wheat and barley, vines and fig trees, pomegranates, olive oil and honey (Deut. 8:8). Micah saw them as places of refuge for the people of God in the last days: "Everyone will sit under their own vine and under their own fig tree, and no one will make them afraid, for the Lord Almighty has spoken" (Micah 4:4).

Jesus alluded to fig trees several times to teach His audience that God blesses His people to bless others. In His parable about a barren fig tree, He taught those who listened about the importance of bearing fruit consistent with repentance (Luke 13:6-9). That's why Jesus cursed the fig tree during Passion Week; it didn't bud fruit to bless others (Mark 11:12-20).

Mr. Nathanael Bartholomew knew from his study of the Scriptures that fig trees were places of deep meditation, hamlets for fruitful devotion to the God of Israel, Who made victorious living possible. That was where His Bible heroes went to study, to pray, and to practice their faith outside the temple. He just followed in their footsteps.

Under that fig tree, Nathanael would have shared his joys and sorrows to the Lord just like David did in the Psalms. He would have shared his victories and failures much like Hezekiah. And he would have shared his certainties and doubts like Micah. All right there, under the fig tree—the fig trees of God. That's why Jesus called him a true Israelite in whom nothing was false.

Nathanael was after God in his life the same way a deer pants after water (Psalm 42:1). And he knew each time he sat under the fig tree to worship, the Lord Almighty would speak to him. This disciple was nothing like his fellow Israelites on the receiving end of Jesus' curse. He not only confessed the God of Abraham, Isaac, and Jacob with his lips, he wanted to bear fruit as well. So, he would, but just under a different covenant—the one that begins by grace through faith alone.

FULL OF PREJUDICE

The very fact that Nathanael practiced his faith sincerely made him think he was better than other people, both personally and spiritually. Right under a fig tree, he might have even read this prophecy from Micah and thought—falsely—that he had God's mind all figured out: "But you, Bethlehem Ephrathah, though you are small among the clans of Judah, out of you will come for me one who will be ruler over Israel, whose origins are from of old, from ancient times" (Micah 5:2).

Thus, the reason he disparaged Nazareth when Philip told him, "We have found the one Moses wrote about in the Law and about whom the prophets also wrote—Jesus of Nazareth, the son of Joseph" (John 1:45).

Nathanael had learned a lot under the fig tree and at the temple, where he cultivated enough biblical intelligence to know that the Messiah was to be born in Bethlehem, not Nazareth. Nothing good has ever come from Nazareth, Nathanael reasoned, particularly concerning the Hope for Israel. He hated that place and let Philip know it. What he did not know was that the Roman census by Caesar Augustus forced Joseph and Mary to leave Nazareth and go to Bethlehem, where Jesus was born (Luke 2:1-4).

Nathanael wasn't privy to that information because he was not God, Whose holy wisdom was even foolishness to people who hunger and thirst after God as he did. As a result, when Philip pointed Nathanael toward Nazareth and mentioned it in the same sentence with the Messiah, his response revealed the nature of his prejudice.

Nazareth was home to zero Messianic prophecies. Nathanael was also familiar with the city's less-than-stellar political reputation. After Herod the Great died in 4 BC, some Jews in the region robbed a Roman armory in

Sepphoris, just four miles outside of Nazareth. As a result, the Romans responded by crucifying thousands of Jews there and in neighboring Galilean towns, including Nazareth.[51] Nathanael had no regard for Nazareth because he equated it with stealing and murder, not with the ushering in of a new way God was going to relate to humanity.

I'm sure he was waiting for an opportunity to scatter, smother, and cover this supposed Christ when he arrived in that terrible place because of all the time he spent under the fig tree studying and praying. Jesus, though, spoke first and schooled him: "When Jesus saw Nathanael approaching, he said of him, 'Here truly is an Israelite in whom there is no deceit'" (John 1:47).

Jesus had him pegged long before their first handshake and wanted Nathanael to know it, continuing, "I saw you while you were still under the fig tree before Philip called you" (John 1:48).

Had I worn the crown, Nathanael would have reaped a piece of my mind: *"Buddy, you think you know the Scriptures? Do you think you know all there is to know about the Messiah just because you happen to pray more than most under fig trees? What makes you think you are better spiritually than other people? Is it your devotional life? Is that what you think? Well, I know everything about you, son of Tolmai, and you are flat out wrong, Donkey Kong."*

The Lord would have been right to speak to him like that. Nathanael deserved it. The Lord chose words of kindness that lead to repentance (Rom. 2:4) instead when He revealed His omniscience to him. Jesus didn't count his trespasses against Nathanael (2 Cor. 5:19).

Consequently, the moment Nathanael left the shade of the fig tree—spiritually speaking—to follow Jesus, the Lord began teaching him that knowledge puffs up, but love builds up (1 Cor. 8:1). He needed to learn that God does indeed smile upon and use people with intense devotion who try to do the right things in their lives. Luke, Andrew, and Barnabas are examples of that. But he also smiles upon and uses folks whose reputations are less-than-noble before encountering the living Christ, much like Matthew.

THE PERSPECTIVE LESSON

With the skill of a masterful spiritual Surgeon, Jesus affirmed and rebuked Nathanael at the same time (John 1:47). He deemed him a truth-teller haplessly incapable of withholding his uninformed opinions on matters of which he was ignorant.

Jesus sought him because He wanted to mold the former and break him of the latter. Without Divine surgery in both areas, Nathanael would have been too judgmental to see people through God's eyes in the mission that Jesus had for him. So, breaking Nathanael of himself was our Savior's only option.

You see, Nathanael needed to learn that Jesus' missional gate has a narrow entryway with a lot of room inside. It has room for Abraham, who pawned his wife off to save himself; the prostitutes of the world like Rahab; the adulterers and adulteresses of the world like David, Solomon, and Mary Magdalene; folks like Isaiah, who didn't have enough sense to put clothes on when preaching; Ezekiel, who was bipolar; Jeremiah, who was too emotional to be coherent. And let us not forget folks like the bloodthirsty Paul and the foul-mouthed Peter.

This son of Tolmai did not think God could work through people who took the fig tree less seriously than he did. And he was entirely wrong. Jesus did not come into this world to make bad people good. Only God is good according to Jesus (Luke 18:19). He came into this world to make people who are dead in their transgressions alive in Christ and new creations. Nathanael was just as dead in his sins as Matthew or Paul, though his violations were internal. He had the malady of personal and spiritual prejudice.

THE PERSPECTIVE CHANGE

In his children's book *The Magician's Nephew*, C.S. Lewis observes, "What you see and what you hear depends a great deal on where you are standing. It also depends on what sort of person you are."[52]

What a character-building lesson for children! Nathanael's childlike faith in Jesus became the catalyst for a new perspective about God's mission in the world. It also showed the depth of his character.

Jesus rebuked the Pharisees often because their hearts were hardened to His Father's purpose and mission in the world. Nathanael's wasn't. After realizing that only the Messiah could look straight into his eyes and educate him on the true meaning of *"el natan,"* he declared, "Rabbi, you are the Son of God; you are the king of Israel" (John 1:49).

After all those days under the fig tree, Nathanael finally understood the Scriptures fully because the Word Who became flesh was staring right at him and giving him a theological education he would never forget. And to the One Who read his heart and mind, Nathanael "capitulated forever."[53] Jesus was now his Teacher (Rabbi) and Messiah (Son of God) and Someone worthy of his submission (King of Israel).

Such an admission required genuine humility from Nathanael at that moment. It meant that he, too, was impoverished of spirit without Jesus (Matt. 5:3). God broke through the darkest cauldrons of his heart. As a result, Nathanael saw himself as Jesus first saw him: in need of a Savior. After the Divine eye surgery, he learned to see people through the eyes of the Savior Himself.

By that confession, Nathanael admitted by default that folks have different transgressions but the same need for Jesus. *Just As I Am, Without One Plea*[54] applied as much to him as it did to Matthew. And it still applies as much to you as it does to me.

LEARNING WHAT HEAVEN WILL LOOK LIKE

Jesus wasn't finished with this disciple yet. He also taught him what Heaven was going to look like: "Very truly I tell you, you will see 'heaven open, and the angels of God ascending and descending on' the Son of Man" (John 1:51).

In the New Testament, the heavens opened only at the baptism of Jesus (Matt. 3:16; Luke 3:21), and in the visions of the apostles regarding their mission in the world (Acts 7:56, 10:11, and Rev. 19:11). In the Old Testament, Jacob caught a similar glimpse (Gen. 28:10). All of these denote communication between Heaven and Earth. Nathanael was privileged enough to be "read in" by Jesus at that moment.

He learned that if God did not move him to missions for people lost without a Savior because they were too proud of their integrity—just like the elder brother in the parable of the prodigal son (Luke 15:25-32)—then his theology was wrong. And if God did not move him to missions for people like the shameful prodigal son, then his theology was false and required editing. Individuals like Luke and Nathanael fill pews in the sanctuary of Heaven, as do people like Zacchaeus and me. Who are we to block those pews with prejudice?

You see, the Gospel is not just for people like the latter who need a radical life change. It is also for people like Nathanael who need a radical perspective change. It is for people who need the Lord. Period.

Can anything good come from Nazareth? Yes, something good can, Nathanael. His name is Jesus. You saw His glory by going inside His discipleship tent and taking your seat in His Divine classroom. You tasted and saw that His figs are good because God made them with the perfect ingredients of infinite kindness, goodness, and unmerited favor. Now, other people can as well.

SOME QUESTIONS TO PONDER BEFORE MOVING ON

1. What is your definition of "prejudice?" In what ways have you made incorrect judgments about people, church, and God? What did you learn?

2. We often judge God by the way He carries out our agenda for the world. Explain.

3. Read Romans 2:1. What do our prejudices reveal about *us* according to the text?

Chapter 8

MATTHEW: THE VILEST OFFENDER WHO TRULY BELIEVED

MY KIDS' PEDIATRICIAN HAS THE special gift of teaching my offspring to do things that he knows will drive me up the wall. He's been engaged in these shenanigans for years, even when they were barely old enough to walk and talk. When he taught them to do the Florida Gators chomp, I decided enough was enough.

Since he has three girls, I vowed before the sun, moon, and stars that I was going to go through any means necessary—including bribery—to find out what drives him bananas. Such an endeavor took quite a spell because he plays his cards very close to his vest.

But while at his home for a moment, he showed me a card he later regretted. He chastised his youngest for playing with something very loud, telling her that he was going to throw *all* of her toys in the trash if she did not silence it. At that moment, I saw the prankster light and decided I had to strike while the iron was hot.

I went straight to Walmart in pursuit of the loudest and vilest toy possible for her to open in front of him on her birthday. I found a terrible one, too: a megaphone with a built-in voice distorter. She smiled brightly at my present on her special day; I certainly did, too, when I saw the abhorred scowl on his face. I became the vilest of toy givers on that day.

GIFT OF GOD

I love the disciple named Matthew because his name means "gift of God." His parents constructed it from two Hebrew words: "mattan," (gift) and "yah(weh)"[55] (God). And if you search the Old Testament for both of these words together in the same sentence, you'll learn that God is quite the Gift-giver.

The most important gift for our discussion of Matthew occurs in Numbers: "From among all the Israelites, I have given <u>the Levites as gifts to Aaron and his sons</u> to do the work at the tent of meeting on behalf of the Israelites and to make atonement for them so that no plague will strike the Israelites when they go near the sanctuary" (Num. 8:19—emphasis mine*)*.

In his account of his calling, Matthew tells us, "As Jesus went on from there, he saw a man named Matthew sitting at the tax collector's booth. 'Follow me,' he told him, and Matthew got up and followed him" (Matt. 9:9).

Mark narrates Matthew's calling for us as well but uses a different name: "As he walked along, he saw Levi son of Alphaeus sitting at a tax collector's booth. 'Follow me,' Jesus told him, and Levi got up and followed him" (Mark 2:14).

Luke does, too: "After this, Jesus went out and saw a tax collector by the name of Levi sitting at his tax booth. 'Follow me,' Jesus said to him, and Levi got up, left everything and followed him" (Luke 5:27-28).

Did you notice that all three narratives denote an identical call and response? When the writers of the Gospels choose to educate their readers about a disciple's calling, they craft their story in a way that shows them what was unique about that person. Or in the case of John and James, what was unique about the brothers. What they wouldn't do is craft the same narrative for two different people. That means Matthew was Levi, and Levi was Matthew.

In the Bible, you don't get the name Levi without being a Levite. They were the hired holy men of Israel. A descendant of the tribe of Benjamin couldn't make sacrifices at the tabernacle or the temple. They had to hand them over to the Levites in charge of worship to do it for them instead. Matthew's blood ancestors had altitudinous callings; both of his names—Matthew and Levi—reflected as much.

Before he took a breath in this world, God had his name already picked out. Even before he was in his mother's womb, the Lord, the Creator of the heavens and the earth, decreed, "There is a disciple that I'm going to name Matthew Levi. He will be one of My gifts to the world, one of My most prized possessions until I come again. People will know his name. And, consequently, they will know My Name because of him."

One problem, though: decreeing Matthew as a gift to the world before birth seems like a perfect oxymoron—much like jumbo shrimp and tight slacks—because he's hardly the vanguard of God's righteousness when we meet him in the Gospels. He's quite the opposite.

Matthew was a Levite in name only. Had he heard his Levitical number to report for temple duty at nine a.m. to serve God and His people on the Day of Atonement, Mr. Matthew Levi would have been a no-show. He only had one primary passion in his life: himself.

THE VILEST OFFENDER

Matthew was the "vilest of offenders who truly <u>didn't</u> believe."[56] He even tells us so, stating that he was "sitting at the tax collector's booth" (Matt. 9:9) when Jesus called him to Himself. As a way of denoting his lack of character before this encounter, he uses the middle voice of the verb "sit."[57] Using it precisely in this way is Matthew's way of telling his readers that he—the subject—is acting in the story reflexively for his benefit.

His booth was more than likely located near a beach of the Sea of Galilee so that he could collect taxes from merchants who were coming into his region from other cities around the lake.[58] He was good at it, too. To line his own pockets, Matthew came up with innovative ways to raise taxes on his fellow Jewish brethren to fatten his wallet.

Tax collectors, or publicans, receive ink twenty-three times in the New Testament. None of them are positive. That's because tax collectors like Matthew worked for the Romans, even though they were Jewish. The Romans demanded a certain amount from them, and what was left over went straight into their pockets. As a result, publicans became quite skilled in extorting their Jewish "neighbors."[59]

Such acts made them not only despised by their fellow "brethren," but also by others who happened to be in town for business. It also made them perfect examples of what it means to have a self-centered view of life. Jesus even referred to them as such: "If you love those who love you, what reward will you get? Are not even the tax collectors doing that?" (Matt. 5:46).

Galileans were blue-collared people who earned their living via the sea and the sweat of their brow in the fields. They were already taxed to the gills by the Romans as well as Herod Antipas. The last thing they needed was some publican named Matthew with his proverbial hands in the tax pot. But that's what they had in this Levitical pariah.

Beating his chest and saying, "Have mercy upon me oh, God a sinner" (Luke 18:13) wasn't in Matthew's verbal arsenal like it was for the publican Jesus mentions in His parable. He had no regard for anything holy, pure, and righteous. Nor did he esteem God's people in a way that is consistent with the character of the God of Israel. A spiritual Levite he was not; the vilest of sinners he most certainly was.

And Matthew wanted to make sure you know that about who he was before he met Jesus. That's why he inserts himself into the narrative. Because without understanding the complete and utter filthiness of sin before God, you will never understand the beauty of His grace.

Show me an individual who thinks his sinful condition is less obtrusive before God than another's, and I will show you someone who does not understand the love and grace of God and what it means to live in it. On the other hand, show me an individual who understands the depth of his dastardly state before regeneration, and I'll show you a person who understands what unmerited favor really means. That's why Matthew didn't mind shouting about his moral bankruptcy before he encountered the forgiving Christ from the rooftops.

WHO TRULY BELIEVED

God makes no mistakes, absolutely none! And the moment Matthew bowed low to leave the tax collectors booth is the exact instant God covered him with righteousness and exalted him. In the next sentence he writes just after his call, Matthew tells us, "While Jesus was having dinner at Matthew's house, many tax collectors and sinners came and ate with him and his disciples. When the Pharisees saw this, they asked his disciples, 'Why does your teacher eat with tax collectors and sinners?' On hearing this, Jesus said, 'It is not the healthy who need a doctor, but the sick'" (Matt. 9:10-12).

My table at home is open to anyone who dares to eat the grub I like to whip up on occasion. But open invitations like mine were not standard in Matthew's time. People were included or excluded in those days based on religious affiliation and ethical norms. Sadducees ate with Sadducees, and Pharisees ate with Pharisees. Moreover, tax collectors were right up there with lepers in the unclean department, so you didn't even think about eating lamb chops with those individuals, not unless you just wanted your relatives and friends to shun you.

Jesus wasn't worried about any of those human-made ethical norms. He accepted Matthew's invitation to dine with him and the rest of his filthy ilk. That Matthew went from a tax farmer to a banquet host immediately isn't a coincidence. It's a miracle. In one instant, he went from being served to serving others. In this case, it was God Himself!

The narrative tells us a lot about God and those who see Him correctly. Matthew only saw his sin; others did, too. But Jesus saw instead what He created him to be: a gift to the world. He started unwrapping him with His benevolent hands and sharing with others the moment he turned from his tax racket to go in the opposite direction.

The religious custodians were too busy murmuring about Matthew to invest in him. Jesus, however, saw value, worth, and treasure. Because He did, the pious ministerial gossips became last, and Matthew became first (Matt. 20:16) at that exact moment. That is why you read his Gospel first in the New Testament and always will. His call from the tax collector's booth to the merciful arms of God illustrates the transformative power of the Gospel of Jesus Christ. It was powerful enough to save a literal wretch like Matthew—and one like me. And we both wrote to tell you the truth about Him and us.

LEST NO MAN SHOULD BOAST

To boast is to speak with "excessive pride and self-satisfaction about one's achievements, possessions, or abilities."[60] People who did this in the Bible regretted it.

For example, Nebuchadnezzar once said, "Is not this the great Babylon I have built as the royal residence, by my mighty power and for the glory of my majesty?" (Dan. 4:30). Just as soon as he finished speaking, God Himself spoke from Heaven and finished the story: "This is what is decreed for you, King Nebuchadnezzar: Your royal authority has been taken from you. You will be driven away from people and will live with the wild animals . . . Seven times will pass by for you until you acknowledge that the Most High is sovereign over all kingdoms on earth and gives them to anyone he wishes" (Dan. 4:31-32).

Matthew knew how Nebuchadnezzar felt; being humbled by the Almighty doesn't soothe the soul of the one who lives low. By their actions, the clerics casting judgmental glances and spouting incredulous barbs lived low also.

They just didn't have the self-evaluation mechanism within them—the Holy Spirit—to admit it.

The writer of the first book in the New Testament did. He knew that instead of condemning him—which Matthew deserved—Jesus encountered him the same way He confronted the blood-thirsty Saul. He shone a light in his face and shouted to his heart, "Live in my love for you, Matthew, because 'my yoke is easy and my burden is light'" (Matt. 11:30).

Matthew had nothing to boast about there at the booth. He could only see himself as Jesus saw him and say, like John Bunyan, "I was sin from the top of my head to the soles of my feet."[61] This publican knew that Jesus' call for him to leave his perch was an invitation to experience the forgiveness and sustaining grace he knew he needed. And equally, Matthew knew that call demonstrated the unconditional love God had for him, the vilest of offenders.

You see, to become great in the Kingdom of God, you must become the least. To see Jesus and His mission in His world rightly, you have to experience the cross before the crown. This publican's knees had to buckle before his deliverance. Your knees do, too. And the moment Matthew rose to a standing position, Jesus started using him. And he will use you also.

Matthew wasted no time fleeing the booth on bended knee. Consequently, Jesus loved him right where he was to get him where He wanted Matthew to be. That was Jesus' mission then. It still is for all who follow Him. And it will be until the end of time. He delights in making gifts for the world out of those who are willing to bend low first.

GRACE PLUS NOTHING

Matthew's story also illustrates what grace plus nothing is all about in the economy of God's redemption program. A.W. Tozer defined the concept the best: "Grace is the good pleasure of God that inclines him to bestow benefits upon the undeserving. It is a self-existent principle inherent in the divine nature and appears to us as a self-caused propensity to pity the wretched, spare the guilty, welcome the outcast, and bring favor to those who were before under just disapprobation."[62]

Matthew's story fits that description. To come to Christ, he could not point to his good works because there were none. Nor could he point out to Jesus his penchant for loving God and neighbor like the rich, young ruler tried to do (Matt. 19:16-22). Matthew could only bow low and leave the booth, an occurrence of repentance "that required nothing short of a miraculous turnaround in his life."[63] All he had to offer Jesus was faith—a trusting conviction that God's kindness exceeds His deserved wrath. And that was good enough for Jesus.

In his epistle to the Ephesians, Paul writes, "For it is by grace you have been saved, through faith—and this is not from yourselves, it is the gift of God—not by works, so that no one can boast" (Eph. 2:8-9).

He learned the truth of that statement personally on the road to Damascus, the avenue where Saul became Paul (Acts 9:1-19). Grace alone covered him; it also changed him. It shaped Paul; it also molded him. It justified him, and it sanctified him.

Matthew learned it personally, too, for the same reasons. That is why his name means "gift of God." It illustrates the unmerited favor of God that comes by grace alone through faith alone. And the moment Matthew turned to Christ by putting his dirty hands into Provident ones, Jesus lifted him with them and made him clean. And his sins, which were too numerous to count, were erased.

THE WISDOM OF GOD IS THE FOOLISHNESS OF MAN

Matthew's story also demonstrates that the very wisdom of God is the complete and utter foolishness of man. When we gain knowledge—whether through formal education or the School of Hard Knocks—we like to boast about it. When I was younger, if I had a dollar for every time I heard someone tell me "when I was your age," I would be a wealthy man. That's because our concept of education and why we learn is built on achievement and "maintaining grounds for boasting."[64]

If charged with the task of ushering in a New Covenant, I would make sure my principal cast of characters had connections in high levels of influence and could balance a balance a checkbook. I would have chosen people like Judas, not Matthew, and told everyone who would listen to do the same. Matthew would have been the last person I would want to write a Gospel that appears first in the New Testament.

God is the exact opposite of me. Paul tells us about how He operates:

> For it is written: "I will destroy the wisdom of the wise; the intelligence of the intelligent I will frustrate." Where is the wise person? Where is the teacher of the law? Where is the philosopher of this age? Has not God made foolish the wisdom of the world? . . . For the foolishness of God is wiser than human wisdom, and the weakness of God is stronger than human strength" (1 Cor. 1:19-20, 25).

He majors in ushering in a New Covenant in people's hearts by using throw-away people who needed no catechism about original sin to know what it is. They lived it.

John Newton would tell you the same thing. He made his living selling people from Africa as slaves in Europe. He needed no preacher to give him an exposition of the Book of Romans to explain sin. Newton's life was the essence of it.

When he turned from his sin and went in the exact opposite direction, he became God's handiwork for unmerited favor. Literally. He bowed low; and there, from that humble and thankful position, he wrote the words, "Amazing grace how sweet the sound."[65] They echoed through the English Parliament when William Wilberforce, who was inspired by them, successfully led the charge to abolish the slave trade in England.[66]

Not too bad for a former slave trader, eh? Newton should have gone to prison; Matthew also. Instead, God freed them from their spiritual prison and then used them mightily to free others from a physical hell they helped to create. That's called grace; and it is, indeed, amazing.

MATTHEW'S MISSION BELL

Can you identify with any of these words: broken, downtrodden, despised, destitute, discarded, denounced, and sinner? Matthew could. He knew all of them by heart because he lived them. But when grace plus nothing in the person of Jesus Christ accepted him right where he was—the tax collector's booth—a radical transformation occurred in Matthew's life. Consequently, he developed a passion for people like lepers (8:1-4, 26:6), a paralytic (9:1-8), an unclean woman (9:20-21), a mute (9:32-33), a Gentile woman severely demon-possessed (15:21-28), and an epileptic (17:15) for a reason. They all knew, like Matthew, what it felt like to be on the receiving end of being discarded by the world; and he wanted them to see that they, too, have value, worth, and merit in God's sight.

Aiming to prove that Jesus is the King of Kings, Matthew steered his Gospel toward those who knew they needed to see Provident royalty that is merciful and equitable at the same time. So, he painted a picture with his words of a King adorned with a crown of thorns hanging on a cross. He signed it with an image of a King Who rose from the dead to make *all* of us clean. Matthew was, after all, highly qualified to paint such a portrait because he knew the dirtiness of sin and the cleanliness of God's mercy.

Yes, Matthew, the vilest offender, was God's gift to the world then and still is now. For within his Gospel lies a beautiful portrait of grace and mercy that meets you right where you are, whether in a tax collector's booth or under a fig tree like Nathanael. And you can only experience that when you relate to God as he did, not like the self-congratulatory religious folk who were mumbling to each other about why Jesus was eating with someone like "him" in the first place.

MATTHEW'S LESSON FOR ALL OF US

Matthew's story from worst to first teaches us that we are in grave danger spiritually when we do not see ourselves as he did on both sides of the cross. His portrait before was ugly; ours is, too. It is worse than we think. But his post-mercy silhouette is beautiful; ours is also. It's better than we think.

The moment we surmise we can graduate from our original condition by our merit is the exact second we become white-washed tombs. Jesus warns us about this, stating, "Woe to you, teachers of the law and Pharisees, you hypocrites! You are like whitewashed tombs, which look beautiful on the outside but on the inside are full of the bones of the dead and everything unclean" (Matt. 23:27).

Unless we see ourselves as Matthew saw himself, we will attend church to be respected by others for being spiritual and "good" instead of attending to worship God for the grace we have received.

When Jesus said the last would be first, and the first will be last, He meant every word of it. You wouldn't have a New Testament and the greatest song ever written if He did not. It's true for us as well. Matthew, John Newton, and the apostle Paul would agree. Do you?

SOME QUESTIONS TO PONDER BEFORE MOVING ON

1. Read Matthew 9:9-13. How might Matthew have seen himself as sick and in need of a doctor?

2. In what ways were the Pharisees sick, even though they didn't realize it?

3. Read Hosea 6:6. How should the Pharisees have treated Matthew?

Chapter 9

THOMAS: THE FIRST DOUBTER AMONG EQUALS

"TALL TALE, DERRICK. THAT'S THE tallest tale you've told in quite a spell. You've really told a whopper. And you've told it mighty well. And in all the years I've traveled on the tall tale telling trail, I've never heard a tall tale teller tell a taller tale." Don't credit me for coming up with that because I did not. Johnny Cash did.[67] But my kids think I did because I sing it to them when I catch them giving me a fish story. And I would prefer it stays that way, okay?

You know what a tall tale is. I've uttered several before but haven't in quite a spell. But those yarns sound like this:

> "Hey, Ethel. Skeeter and I went fishing down at the Stick Marsh, and we caught a fish so big that the boat nearly sank when we pulled it in."

> "Well, where is it?"

> "We had to throw it back because it was over the size limit."

We don't limit our tall tales to fish stories that we tell Ethel either. They are ingrained in our Americana consciousness. If you ask folks in Minnesota or Wisconsin about Paul Bunyan, they might try to convince you that he once ate fifty pancakes in one minute. Some in the Pacific Northwest will swear to you that they've seen Sasquatch up close and personal. I'll bet you can't even name a town in the United States whose folklore doesn't include some female ghost or apparition who's been reportedly looking for her long-lost love at a particular spot. Doubt lies on the other side of tales like these because if we take them at face value, they are hard to believe. That's why we doubt them, even when told mighty well.

There is one disciple who gets singled out for his penchant for doubt. His name is Thomas. We call him Doubting Thomas for a reason. When the disciples told him Jesus had risen from the dead, his response was, "You've really told a whopper this time, and you've told it mighty well."

BORN TO DOUBT

On three occasions in his Gospel, John tells us that Thomas also went by the name of Didymus (11:16, 20:24, and 21:2). The latter means "twin," or "double."[68] As a result, the likelihood that he had a twin brother is highly probable. But the origins of his predisposition for doubting comes via the symbolic meaning of his name. Thomas was double, or twinned, in his thinking patterns.

James tells us this about double-mindedness: "The one who doubts is like a wave of the sea, blown and tossed by the wind. That person should not expect to receive anything from the Lord. Such a person is double-minded and unstable in all they do" (Jas. 1:6-8).

An individual is unstable if he is divided against himself internally in nearly everything he does. There can be no doubt—pun intended—that such a description fits Thomas like a glove. It's why he can say, "Let's die with him" one day (John 11:16), and "Unless I see nail-marks, fellas, I will not believe" on another (John 20:25). It's also why he can question Jesus about being the only way to Heaven in one breath (John 14:5) and then utter, "My Lord and my God" in another (John 20:28). Thomas believed his doubts and had no trouble doubting his beliefs.[69] He was twin-minded after all. And his name, Thomas called Didymus, proved it.

THE FIRST AMONG EQUALS

Thomas has, unfortunately, developed a reputation within Christian circles over the last two thousand years as being *the* disciple who doubted. That tends to happen when distinguished individuals like Caravaggio, a fifteenth-century Italian painter, labels the canvas he made of him *The Incredulity of Saint Thomas*.[70]

Dale Carnegie saw him through a similar lens: "Almost all the progress ever made in human thought has been made by the Doubting Thomases, the questioners, the challengers, and the show-me crowd."[71]

The truth is all of the disciples doubted Jesus, not just Thomas. I still question my Lord and God when He demands me to trust Him with what my mind can't conceive or solve. Doubt is as old and familiar now as it was in the Garden of Eden.

On fourteen occasions in the Gospels, the doubts of the disciples are in full view. Four of them relate to the resurrection. In Matthew's Gospel, the disciples are instructed to go to a mountain to find Jesus. When they did, some of them worshipped, and others doubted (Matt. 28:17). Luke even records that they thought they had seen a ghost (Luke 24:37).

But my favorite episode of raising eyebrows at God's actions occurs when Mary Magdalene, Joanna, and Mary, the mother of Jesus, inform the disciples that Jesus is alive. To which they respond in unison that it was a bunch of nonsense (Luke 24:11).

In the language of the New Testament, "nonsense" evokes the ideas of idle talk, babbling, and delirium.[72] Does that sound like a group of folks whose faith was a "bulwark never failing"?[73] So, don't believe for a second that Thomas was the sole doubter. He wasn't. He happens to be the first doubter among equals, the one who has been singled out for saying, "Yeah, right."

A long time ago in a perfect garden, a serpent slithered right up to Adam and Eve and said, "Did God really say, 'You must not eat from any tree in the garden'?" (Gen. 3:1).

Isn't it interesting that the first Satanic attack in the Bible came from the serpent's fiery dart of doubt about what God had spoken and made crystal clear? He wanted Adam and Eve to disbelieve God's word; he wants us to scruple it as well.

DOUBT IS DOUBT

In ancient Greece, the Sophists suspended their judgment when investigating claims too difficult to take at face value.[74] Their skepticism was much different than ours. We suspend judgment without investigation, only saying, "Oh really?"

Unfortunately, though, skeptics in our world like to play their doubt cards under deceptive veils of intellectualism. When they do, they often go something like this: "Derrick, you don't honestly expect me to believe that what the Bible says about Jesus being the only way to Heaven is truthful, do you? Isn't that how John and the rest of the New Testament writers interpreted what He said?"

Some creative ones might even put their doubts and denials to tune and sell them to the masses like this one did:

> *Paul is making me nervous*
> *Paul is making me scared*
> *Walk into this room and swaggers*
> *Like he's God's own messenger*
> *Changed the name of my brother*
> *Changed the things that he said*
> *Says he speaks to him*
> *But he never even knew the man.*
>
> *Will it be the end?*
> *Or is he still ascending?*
> *But if he's all you say*
> *Would he fly from heaven*
> *To this world again.*[75]

Our doubts might sound like this:

"God, do you love me unconditionally?"

"Will you provide for my family and me, Lord? I'm having a hard time trusting You will, even though I know I should."

"Lord Jesus, do You have a plan for me? I'm having difficulty discovering it if you do."

"My sins are many, Lord, because I've made some abominable choices in my life. Can you forgive them and remember them no more, especially since the probability is high that I will make more of them at some point?"

Be advised, however, that all forms of doubt come straight from the Garden of Eden. When you and I doubt, the stories of serpents, gardens, choices, and Thomas are no longer just accounts of antiquity stored on the old pages of the Holy Writ. They are real and personal.

HAS ANYONE SEEN THOMAS?

Thomas gets labeled "the doubter" among the other "doubting" disciples because he was not in as close of fellowship with Jesus as the others. John tells us:

> On the evening of that first day of the week, when the disciples were together, with the doors locked for fear of the Jewish leaders, Jesus came and stood among them and said, "Peace be with you!" After he said this, he showed them his hands and side. The disciples were overjoyed when they saw the Lord ... Now Thomas (also known as Didymus), one of the Twelve, was not with the disciples when Jesus came" (John 20:19-20, 24).

That John chose to inform his audience that Thomas was absent when Jesus first appeared to them is crucial considering what follows next: "So the other disciples told him, 'We have seen the Lord'" (John 20:25).

Thomas had to be summoned back into the fold by the others so that he could have a conversation with the resurrected Jesus. The implication is obvious. Thomas doubted the resurrection more than the others because he was not present, even though he should have been.

From prison, Paul told the church in Philippi that the greatest desire of his heart was to know Christ and the "fellowship of his sufferings" (Phil. 3:10). Those present just before Christ appeared knew all about that; thus, the reason they had the door bolted shut. Thomas didn't because he was not there.

There is a direct correlation between doubt and lack of fellowship with God and His people. Show me a professing follower of Jesus who loses the doubt battle and starts singing the serpent's garden song, and I will show you a defeated individual who is like chaff blowing in the wind (Psalm 1:4). On the other hand, show me a person who delights in God daily and makes fellowship with His people a priority, and I will show you someone who's grounded and bears genuine spiritual fruit (Psalm 1:1-3).

Moreover, fellowship with the resurrected Lord and with His people equates to faith, belief, certainty, and rest in God's character. That's how Christian faith flourishes; it's why we sing *Blessed Be the Tie that Binds*[76] and why we hear preachers say things like this on Sunday mornings: "I would rather be chained in a dungeon, wrist to wrist with a Christian, than to live forever with the wicked in the sunshine of happiness."[77]

On the contrary, one lacking fellowship with Him and with others swims in the Bermuda Triangle of doubt that brings hopelessness, despair, and a lack of joy. May we learn from Thomas' absence so that we don't repeat his errors.

The moment we believe our accuser is truthful is, unfortunately, the exact occasion we have stopped listening to the One Who died to remove our sins and cast them as far away as the east from the west (Psalm 103:12). But when we choose to stop doubting and believe our Redeemer, thoughts like these flow through our minds: "Jesus, I know You love and care for me. I believe You because I know Your nature is good and kind. Furthermore, I believe that Your mercies are new every morning because Your Word says they are (Lam. 3:22-23). So, I claim them, therefore, for my family and myself right now."

Doubting God is as common for us as breathing because we are human. We all doubt as Thomas did. He didn't continue residing there, though, as we will see. Neither should we.

WITH GREAT DOUBTS CAME GREATER REVELATIONS

The God of the Bible tends to respond to great doubts with greater revelations of His character. While eavesdropping on Abraham's conversation with the three messengers of the Lord, Sarah laughed in a "display of incredulity"[78] when she heard the prophecy that she would bare a son within a year (Gen. 18:10-12). Her snicker prompted this question from the Divine: "Is anything too hard for the Lord?" (Gen. 18:14).

Moses doubted his calling to lead Israel out of Egypt (Exod. 3:11); he didn't after the waters parted. Habakkuk questioned God's justice (Hab. 1:2-4); he didn't after the Lord Himself responded to his complaints. Thomas was no exception to the Lord's method for doubt-busting. He was just the next in line, another soul prone to doubt that God had to show just how powerful He is to get him to believe.

Every single time Thomas doubted, Jesus responded with a revelation of Who He was—and still is—that was greater than any of his doubts. Jesus' love was so great for Thomas that He revealed the highest aspects of His character in all the New Testament to the one disciple we single out for being the greatest doubter!

Jesus revealed his exclusivity to Thomas: "Thomas said to him, 'Lord we don't know where you are going, so how can we know the way?' Jesus answered: 'I am the way and the truth and the life. No one comes to the Father except through me'" (John 14:5-6).

Humanity is lost, not found. We are prone to disbelief, not faith. According to these words, apart from an exclusive faith relationship with the Jesus Christ of the Gospels—and that representation of Jesus Christ only—people remain lost and will enter into eternity separated from Him when they die. Church attendance or activity makes no difference to Him, no matter how high the profile. Just ask Caiaphas the High Priest and the rest of his holy warriors who beseeched Pilate to crucify Jesus even after His beating, courtesy of a Roman flagrum[79] that ripped his flesh apart.

What matters to Him is an exclusive faith relationship that is evidenced by the fruit of the Spirit. That was true then. It is right now because the truth is the truth, regardless of which way the wind of culture blows or what anybody tells you to believe.

And Jesus revealed that to the doubter named Thomas. He did not tell him that He was one option among many. He pronounced to him that He was the only Way to paradise. The issue is whether you doubt that or believe it and make life decisions because of it. That was the issue then. That is the matter now at hand. Jesus loved Thomas enough to tell him that so you could read his conversation with him in the New Testament.

He also revealed his Deity to him: "Unless I see the nail marks in his hands and put my finger where the nails were, and put my hand into his side, I will not believe . . . Then he said to Thomas, 'Put your finger here; see my hands. Reach out your hand and put it into my side. Stop doubting and believe.' And Thomas said to him, 'My Lord and My God" (John 20:25, 27-28).

Lord means "Master."[80] Notice title is used in the same sentence with God in relationship to Jesus Christ. The only time both of those words appear in the same sentence about Jesus in the Gospels is right here in Thomas' confession. Consequently, like Matthew, the last became the first in one instant. He also became the most significant theologian. That is the power of His love, grace, mercy, and truth that meets all of us right where we are to take us to where Jesus wants us to be.

HONEST DOUBTS AND BELIEVING WITHOUT SEEING

After Thomas surrendered his doubts and faith prevailed, Jesus said to him, "Because you have seen me, you believed; blessed are those who have not seen and yet have believed" (John 20:29).

Over the years, theologians devoted much ink to what Jesus meant when He said this. For some, these words are a gentle rebuke aimed at Thomas for having to see before he believed.[81] Others have suggested that Jesus' words here should be interpreted more as a statement of how faith and joy relate to each other.[82] In other words, "joyful and fulfilled" are those who trust without needing tangible evidence to do so.

The latter view makes the most sense in light of the material in John's Gospel. The disciples put their faith in Jesus after He turned the water into wine in Cana (John 2:11). The woman at the well dropped her jar to tell her native Samaritans about Jesus after He gave her a biographical sketch of her life from His Divine perspective (John 4:39). And Lazarus' sister Mary confessed that Jesus was the Christ after her brother shook off his grave clothes (John 11:27).

All of the aforementioned found peace when Christ met them right where they were, Thomas included. They were not looking for a loophole to justify their persistence in unbelief; they wanted to believe. None of these wished to live content with darkness; they craved the light of Jesus.[83] So He gave them a healthy portion of it.

Had Thomas believed before seeing, his soul would have been as still as a lake surrounded by tall oaks. It wasn't. Ours usually isn't either in times of crisis. While He meets us where we are, God's not satisfied that we stay there very long. Jesus wasn't satiated with where Thomas was. He wanted him to believe just because He is God, so Thomas' soul would be at rest in the Almighty, the object of his delight and happiness. The same is true for us.

FROM DOUBTER TO CONVINCED WITNESS

By faith, Thomas believed. As a result, his "weaknesses were turned to strengths" (Heb. 11:34). Jesus also made him into the exact opposite of who he used to be. He went from being a sincere but heart-troubled doubter to one of the most convinced and confident witnesses to the resurrected Christ in the history of Christianity.

Fortunately, Thomas is one of the few disciples about whom is written more about his life outside of the New Testament than inside it. The church historian Eusebius of Caesarea traced his missionary endeavors to Parthia (modern-day Northern Iraq) and India, where he lived in a cave on a mountain for seven years.[84] There, Thomas converted numerous individuals to Christ. Some churches still stand today in India precisely because of his influence.[85]

The soldiers of a local Hindu priest captured Thomas and tried to fry him on calescent plates. Thomas would not die. Then, they threw him into a fiery furnace, and he still would not die.[86]

Thomas died later courtesy of someone spearing him for not renouncing the Lord Who revealed His character to him amid his doubts. He would not deny "the Way, the Truth, and the Life." That is because Jesus loved him; this Thomas knew.[87] For the Bible and the Lord Jesus Himself told him so, with nail-scarred hands and feet to prove it.

SOME QUESTIONS TO PONDER BEFORE MOVING ON

1. Read Mark 9:23-25. In what areas of your life does unbelief exist? Why?

2. Read James 1:5-8. Why does James caution us about praying doublemindedly in these verses? In what areas of your life do you need confident, heavenly wisdom?

3. Read Psalm 138:8. How might one who doubts that God is just be inclined to seek revenge? In what ways can you trust God when you're tempted to take revenge?

Chapter 10
THE ZEALOT'S CROSS

GROWING UP IN THE BUCKLE of the Bible Belt, I learned that you can't run for the political office of dog catcher in that part of our nation without publicly affirming that you are an Evangelical Christian.

My first real experience with one happened when I was fifteen. Ted was his name, and he was my barber. That's right. I used to be a man with hair on top of my head until God decided He wanted to give me the permanent horseshoe look at no charge.

Ted always provided patrons of age with a free shave if natural genetics dictated such a benevolent act of customer service. Mine did at fifteen. And I will never forget that day as long as I live. It was the day Mr. Two-Bits decided to combine his enthusiastic passion for free customer service with his ardent love for Evangelical Christianity at the same time!

First came the Johnny Cash black cape that barbers put on you to prevent your hair from getting all over you and making you itch like Lassie with flees. Then came the shaving cream. The whole exercise went downhill really quickly when he pulled out his razor from his Barbicide Disinfecting Jar.

That cutting device did not look like a razor to me. No, sir! It looked like a machete, mainly since I was already on the barber's gurney. Right before he put his sword to my neck, Ted started right in with his rhapsodic Gospel presentation: "Derrick. If you died today, are you prepared to meet your Maker?"

You've never seen a teenager so scared in his life. I wanted to get out of that chair as fast as Dale Earnhardt, Jr., in the Sun Pass Lane on the 528 in Orlando driving his 1978 Ford Pinto because he is broke and cannot afford to pay the toll. That is probably not the best way to begin a zealous Gospel presentation, not unless you want to scare people into believing. Literally.

There is an obscure disciple mentioned only four times in the New Testament. He has no speaking parts or acts of service. If you blink, you miss him. But I would not gloss over him if I were you. He is one of the most salient disciples, whose worldview before Jesus called him applies to us the most specifically because of the cultural issues going on in our nation right now and how they relate to our faith. His name was Simon the Zealot.

A DANGEROUS ZEAL

When the word "zeal" appears in modern translations of the Bible, it usually denotes the Hebrew concepts of jealousy or envy.[88] God's zeal is good because *He* is good. He seeks exclusive relationships with His people and will do anything and everything pure to bring them about. It's the quality that caused Almighty God to introduce Immanuel to the world to save it (Isa. 9:7).

But when jealousy and envy are the impetus for what we think are "righteous" actions, sin isn't far behind. We're not God, nor are we holy based on our merit. Look no further than King Saul. His successor, David, traced a three-year famine to Saul's zealotry that resulted in the slaughter of the Gibeonites (2 Sam. 21:1-2).

In the New Testament, Jesus' jealousy and envy for His Father's house resulted in Him doing a good cleaning of it, but not with mops and brooms. He edulcorated it with a whip because the money changers exploited people under the guise of serving God. Consequently, they had defiled it (John 2:13-17). Usually, though, zeal denotes passion, concern, eagerness, and an attitude of deep commitment to a person or a cause.[89]

Both of these concepts fit Simon the Zealot better than a tailored three-piece suit from Jos. A. Bank. The Zealots were a group of Jews who formed during the time of the New Testament from nostalgia. During the time between the Testaments, there was a zealous and holy crusader named Judas Maccabeus. We have him to thank for the apocryphal books 1-4 Maccabees.

The pagan Greeks occupied the Holy Land and desecrated the temple and everything holy. Judas got sick and tired of it. As a result, he led a forceful and aggressive revolt because of all the paganism he saw in the land. Though outnumbered and not equipped with sufficient battle weaponry, Mr. Maccabeus was victorious. You'd never have heard of the word *Hanukkah* if he wasn't. That's precisely why Jews celebrate it today.[90]

The Zealots' problem was with the Romans, not the Greeks. They believed the same zealous method Judas Maccabeus used against the Greeks would work against the Romans. So, they formed a political party and tried to do it. One problem, though: the Zealots didn't constitute as a political party until a priest by the name of Eleazar refused to offer sacrifices devoted to Roman emperors—something the chief priests and Pharisees were fine with—until 67-68 AD.[91] How, then, can Luke refer to him as "Simon who was called the Zealot" in one place (Luke 6:15) and "Simon *the* Zealot" in another (Acts 1:13)?

The answer is straightforward: the Gospel writers reference him by a characterizing name, not a technical one. Simon's intense love for his God, land, and people defined who he was as a person. He thought like his ancestor Judas Maccabeus and would have been proud of Eleazar's "enough is enough" stand against the Romans. He was nothing like his compromised Jewish brethren, who feared a military boot on their necks if they didn't make sacrifices to appease them.

Consider Josephus' words about those who thought and acted like Simon: "These men (Zealots) agree in all other things with the Pharisaic notions, but they have an inviolable attachment to liberty, and say that God is to be their only Ruler and Lord."[92]

Do those words sound familiar? They should, most especially if you run in Evangelical Christian circles. They certainly give the whole "what has been done will be done again" and "there is nothing new under the sun" quotable paradigm (Eccl. 1:9) more of a prophetic tone, don't they?

You see, like Patrick Henry, Simon the Zealot would have shouted, "Give me liberty or give me death"[93] to every religious Jew from every mountain because of the rise of the paganism within his land. There was one big problem, though: the Romans were a well-built war machine with twenty times the might of the Greeks. Judas Maccabeus would not have stood a chance against them physically. Simon, "the Zealot," wouldn't either.

A DANGEROUS OUTLOOK

In his book *The Great Divorce,* C.S. Lewis observes:

> There have been men before now who got so interested in proving the existence of God that they came to care nothing for God Himself . . . as if the good Lord had nothing to do but exist! . . . It is the subtlest of all the snares . . . Every poet and musician and artist, but for Grace, is drawn away from love of the thing he tells, to love of the telling till, down in Deep Hell, they cannot be interested in God at all but only in what they say about Him . . . and become interested in their own personalities and then in nothing but their own reputations.[94]

That's how the Pharisees and religious elite chose to practice their faith. They cared nothing for the substance of it at all—only in what it could do for them and how they were perceived. Consequently, they learned the surest way to preserve their reputations and identity was to do whatever the Romans wanted.

But Simon and the rest of his zealous brethren were molded from a different cloth. Pleasing God mattered to the Zealots; ameliorating the Romans didn't. Those of Simon's ilk saw them as pagan enemies of God, opposed to everything holy, righteous, and pure. As a result, they wanted to fight them with daggers—literally, I might add—to restore their land to the way their founding fathers wanted it to be. That's a polite way of saying they were terrorists.[95]

In Luke's Gospel, we read, "In those days Caesar Augustus issued a decree that a census should be taken of the entire Roman world [that included the Holy Land]. (This was the first census that took place while Quirinius was governor of Syria) . . . So Joseph also went up from the town of Nazareth in Galilee to Judea" (Luke 2:1-4).

Simon would not have made a beeline to his hometown to register for this census. He was bitterly opposed to the threatened increase of taxation and had enough of it. Instead, you might have heard him say something like, "Taxation without representation. We should not take this without a fight. We have got to do something about this by whatever means is necessary. If we do not, then our land will become 'godless' and more and more corrupt. I refuse to register for this census. 'Give me liberty, or give me death.'"[96]

Simon would have then fled to Galilee or the Golan Heights in Northern Israel because the Zealots lived in the mountainous caves of those areas. In one of them, the leaders would have met and hatched a plan that might have sounded something like this: "When we see them coming, we will expel them from this land by force. When we finish, we will proceed to the temple and forcibly remove those Romans as well. It worked for Judas Maccabeus against the Greeks. It will work for us against the Romans."

What he would have hated to hear at that precise moment were these words of heavenly wisdom from his Maker: "Put your sword back in its place," Jesus said to him, "for all who draw the sword will die by the sword. Do you think I cannot call on my Father, and he will at once put at my disposal more than twelve legions of angels?" (Matt. 26:52-53).

The thought never occurred to Simon the Zealot and the rest of his holy crusaders that the specific reason the Romans were occupying the land and threatening to unravel everything sacred had something to do with them.

The Zealots were not as chaste as they thought they were and wanted to be perceived by others.

God set Israel apart—Zealots included—to be a fertile vineyard for the world, not a sword. But instead of producing good grapes, they produced bitter fruit not suitable for consumption. Instead of being the Balm of Gilead for their world, they were the thistle of it. God looked for righteousness in them but saw only "bloodshed" and heard only "cries of distress" (Isa. 5:7).

Here's the point: had Simon and his daggermen understood holiness, they would have zealously labored to win the cultural battle against "the pagans" like this: "If my people, who are called by my name, will humble themselves and pray and seek my face and turn from their wicked ways, then I will hear from heaven, and I will forgive their sin and will heal their land" (2 Chron. 7:14).

They didn't, choosing the sword instead because they lacked faith in the God of Abraham, Isaac, and Jacob to control the outcome of a cultural situation. Had they made prayer their greatest weapon, the Zealots would have looked at themselves first and taken the plank out of their eye so they could see clearly (Matt. 7:3).

Had they had enough faith to do some internal investigation, they would have not only repented; they would have also seen the Romans in a light much more consistent with God's character and mission in the world. Instead of enemies, they would have seen the Romans occupying their land as people who needed to know their God the way they did.

That was too hard for them. Such a perspective meant they had to trust God to win the culture war one heart at a time. The Zealots saw no need to pray for their enemies and love them into the Kingdom (Matt. 5:43-48). They wanted to win the culture war against the pagans at all costs. Consequently, they did not care one bit about the spiritual condition of the very people they were called to shine the light of the Gospel to in the first place.

THE MESSIAH'S SWORD AND CROSS

This Zealot could have slung daggers with the best of them. But so could Jesus. His weren't crafted from iron, though. They were was crafted from love, a love forged in the hallowed inferno of anguish and substitution at Calvary. And, consequently, He conquered Simon the same way a shepherd does who leaves ninety-nine sheep to find the one who went awry and astray (Luke 15:4).

Though the Scriptures are silent about how Jesus called him, I would not be surprised if Simon told me when I get to Heaven that the Lord sought him out in a cave in Northern Israel. God tends to do that seeking thing in our lives, doesn't He? After Jesus called him, our Lord captured his heart the same way he conquers ours today: through Calvary.

While exiled at Saint Helena towards the end of his life, Napoleon Bonaparte had this to say about Jesus' ability to subdue the human heart:

> Everything in him astonishes me. His Spirit overawes me, and his will confounds me. Between him and everyone else in the world, there is no possible term of comparison. He is truly a being by himself. His ideas and his sentiments, the truths which he announces, his manner of convincing, are not explained either by human organization or by the nature of things. His birth, and the history of his life; the profundity of his doctrines which grapples the mightiest difficulties, and which is, of those difficulties, the most admirable solution; his gospel, his apparition, his empire, his march across the ages and the realms, everything is to me a prodigy, a mystery insoluble, which plunges me into a reverie from which I cannot escape, a mystery which is there before my eyes, a mystery which I can neither deny nor explain.[97]

Only God knows if Napoleon's understanding of Jesus created a metamorphosis in his heart. Simon the Zealot, however, is different because he was a disciple. The moment Simon left the daggers behind in the cave to follow Jesus, his crusading mission in the world changed. Calvary was going to be his new crusade. Jesus, through His Spirit, was going to teach him how to show others to be conquered by Calvary the same way he was.

He was going to teach Simon that he was worse than he thought he was. Jesus did not need to face execution at Calvary otherwise. But because he did, Simon—and I—can call on the name of the Lord and be saved, even though we punctured His veins. If Simon's new mission was to be successful, Jesus had to get him to look at the cross and think about the radical demands of forgiveness he was called to disperse in light of the mercy he freely received.

THE ZEALOT'S NEW CRUSADE

Jesus forced Simon the Zealot to be on the same team with a Jewish man who lived like a pagan named Matthew. Think about that for a moment. Our Lord forced him into covenant relationship with an individual who stood for nothing holy in his life, did not respect God's people, and made his living by exploiting them entirely for his benefit. Simon and Matthew were natural enemies for good reasons. But they entered into a relationship with the Messiah in the same way: through Calvary and by grace through faith alone.

Neither had anything to boast about before the cross. But they had one thing in common after it. Once they called Jesus' name, God remembered their sins no more (Heb. 8:12). Neither did He remain mindful of the sins of the other disciples. He doesn't remember ours either.

Carrying that cross—and that cross alone—was to be Simon's new crusade in his world. It wasn't an impotent cross either. At this cross, he didn't sing, "I had to investigate to make sure I understood and then I saw the light by my own best estimation." He sang, "Mercy there was great and grace was free."[98] And Jesus commissioned him to sing the same song to those in Beirut whom he preached the Gospel to after Christ's ascension.[99]

Nor was it a consumer's cross. Jesus didn't commission him to work the Christian angle when it benefited him. He called the Zealot to carry Calvary to the world because he experienced it firsthand.

And Simon was not commissioned to hoist an angry cross either. Jesus did not call him to show the cross to the masses and shout, "You did this to Jesus, you pagans!" He was commissioned to say, "We all need this" because we've all contributed to the murder of God by our hands and are still loved mightily by Him.

Calvary was the Messiah's answer to Simon the Zealot's culture war. It is His answer to ours now. Furthermore, it will be His answer for every culture everywhere on Earth until He returns in the future in all His glory. Calvary, not condemnation, is the Balm of Gilead for the world. The Zealot needed to learn that—just as we do.

SOME QUESTIONS TO PONDER BEFORE MOVING ON

1. Read Matthew 26:52. What was Jesus trying to teach Peter? How might we apply this to interpersonal or church conflict? What is an honorable way to deal with conflict?

2. Read Matthew 7:1-5. How can we see issues in our culture clearly from God's perspective according to the text?

3. Read 1 John 1:6-7. What did Simon and Matthew have in common in light of these verses? How can we learn about God's nature and character through relationships?

Chapter 11

JAMES, THE SON OF ALPHAEUS

A TOMB WAS ERECTED IN 1931 at Arlington National Cemetery in Washington, DC, with this inscription: "HERE RESTS IN HONORED GLORY AN AMERICAN SOLDIER KNOWN BUT TO GOD."[100]

More than one heroic soldier rests in that sacred tomb. And because they all lived and died for something greater than themselves, they received the Medal of Honor and Victoria Cross posthumously. It is the Tomb of the Unknown Soldier, a monument to the scores of unidentified soldiers who have fought and died for our country.

The title for the most enigmatic person preserved on the pages of the Bible goes to Melchizedek. He was the king of Salem—the city you know as Jerusalem—and the priest of the Most High God who blessed Abraham (Gen. 14:18-20). He gets plenty of press in the book of Hebrews, too. Consider these clippings for example: "Our forerunner, Jesus, has entered on our behalf. He has become a high priest forever in the order of Melchizedek . . . [He was] Without father or mother, without genealogy, without beginning of days or end of life, resembling the Son of God, he remains a priest forever" (Heb. 6:20, 7:3).

I'd say that an individual who blessed Abraham and is a direct priestly ancestor of our Lord Jesus Christ—if not an actual appearing of Him in the Old Testament—is enough to qualify him as the most heroic, faithful, and enigmatic person to adorn the pages of the Bible. Wouldn't you?

Next on the list is a disciple whose character traits, personal background, strengths, and weaknesses are dense in the Gospels. Like Simon the Zealot, he had no speaking parts or acts of service. And if you blink or yawn while reading the Gospels, you might miss him. His name was James. Don't confuse him with James, the brother of John and son of Zebedee, either. He's not the same person.

The Synoptic writers deem this mysterious James "the son of Alphaeus" (Matt. 10:3; Mark 3:18; Luke 6:15). Of these writers, Mark is the lone author who refers to him with the modifying Greek clause *tou mikrou*. Translators for the New International Version—the English version I've used for this book—render this genitive clause as James "the Younger" (Mark 15:45). On the other hand, other translators of popular English versions (KJV, NKJV, NASB) interpret it as James "the Less." Both inferences are right. The modifier can mean "little, small, of least importance, insignificant, and humble."[101] It can also translate as "the younger."[102]

John MacArthur wrestled with this nomenclature issue in his excellent work on the disciples and argued the clause most likely refers to both his age <u>and</u> influence, writing: "It is probably true that he was younger than the other James" and that "his distinguishing mark was his obscurity."[103] I agree with him because Mark references him briefly in this manner—along with his brother and sister—to establish the validity of their mother, Mary, as a witness to the crucifixion of Jesus. This "little James" then exits stage right and disappears.[104]

JUST WHO WAS THAT MASKED MAN, ANYWAY?

My parents used to listen to *The Lone Ranger* on the radio as children. I used to watch him on television. The only reason I tuned in was to see if the episode that garnered my attention on that day would be the one where he was unmasked for the whole world to see. Every episode disappointed me because the mask remained when the credits began to roll. Thus the reason for the phrase, "Just who was that masked man, anyway?"[105]

That's James the Less for you: The Lone Ranger of the New Testament Disciples. You'll have an easier time ordering an authentic diamond from a television infomercial for three easy payments of $5.99 than you will have to try to unmask him.

Mark tells us that Levi's (Matthew's) father was also named Alphaeus (Mark 2:14). That could mean that James was Matthew's brother. The recovering tax addict alludes to this possibility, listing himself just before James, the son of Alphaeus (Matt. 10:3). There is some precedent for this in his Gospel. On two occasions, he puts Andrew after Peter and James after John before telling his readers that both sets were brothers (Matt. 4:18-22, 10:2). If this James was his brother, why wouldn't he say so?

To further complicate the problem, Mark puts Thomas between Matthew and James; but he also separates Peter from Andrew, who are known brothers (Mark 3:16-18). Luke also puts Thomas between Matthew and James, but he tells us Peter and Andrew were brothers (Luke 6:14-15). So, the Synoptic writers are not much help if you're trying to unmask him either.

Another possibility is that James' father was also named Alphaeus, but unrelated to Matthew. It was a common name in those days. Since it has the same Aramaic root as the name Clopas, James' mother was quite possibly the "Mary, wife of Clopas" John references (John 19:25).

I favor this line of thinking; I wouldn't shout it from the rooftops, though. We don't know. Guessing is our only option. What we do know for sure about Alphaeus' son is he rests in the Gospels in honored glory as one divinely chosen to help usher in a New Covenant: a man who was known fully only by God. And that's okay because we can still glean a couple of principles from this masked disciple.

DIVINELY CHOSEN ON A MOUNTAIN

Even though we know little about him, Jesus divinely chose James, the son of Alphaeus, after communing with His Heavenly Father on a mountain. Just why He did is a mystery we are not meant to understand.

As a result, when the God of the universe works in unfamiliar ways—and for reasons only known to Him—we shouldn't fret. Neither should we try to figure out why He acted in such a manner. If we do, we'll be attempting to "get the heavens into our heads," and "it is our heads that will split."[106]

Instead, we should, like Isaiah, learn to rest in this truth from God Almighty: "As the heavens are higher than the earth, so are my ways higher than your ways and my thoughts than your thoughts" (Isa. 55:9).

God's higher ways should point us to the need for faith in Him, an allegiance that is beautiful because it forces us to admit that He is God and we are not. Such a confession implies that lack of information isn't grounds for unbelief. It forces us to believe God is good, and He cares, even when our questions go unanswered. We can be assured that the Almighty has good reasons for not answering us now. And it beckons us to maintain fellowship with the One Who is both set apart and personal at the same time.

In essence, the inclusion of this James in the disciples' list is an illustration of what resting on the higher ways of God is all about. His very presence in it forces us to conclude God Himself is, at times, mysterious. We must therefore be content with Him when He chooses to be. Just the mentioning of this little-known son of Alphaeus suggests we must crown Jesus as Lord and dethrone ourselves. James' place among the disciples invites us inside the tent as well to dwell with the One Whose omniscience can be trusted.

EMBRACING MYSTERY

I love conspiracy theories as much as anyone. I've spent half my life trying to unravel the mystery that is the assassination of John Fitzgerald Kennedy. It's an enigma I enjoy trying to solve because much of the circumstances of his death have been kept secret in my view. As a result, his death remains, to this day, unexplained primarily to this JFK conspiracy theorist's satisfaction.

That's how we usually define the term *mystery*: something not understood fully that usually has a secretive quality or dimension to it. Biblical mysteries, however, work a little bit different. They are, indeed, hidden things. But they are also some of God's most important methods for governing the righteous that just so happen to be imperceivable to the wicked.[107]

Consider Daniel, for example. He understood esoteric symbols that Nebuchadnezzar did not: mysteries revealed to him by God to demonstrate that His kingdom will stand forever (Dan. 2). Paul even embraced mystery in the Book of Ephesians, a book that is the apostle's theological tractate on the supernatural enigma that is the inclusion of the Gentiles as an equal part of God's covenant people made possible by Jesus' atonement.[108]

The God of the Bible employs Divine mysteries as part of His benevolent plans for governing His people. They emphasize His omniscience, sovereignty, and grace at the same time and in the same relationship. As a result, if Paul can use them as occasions to pray for others to be "filled to the measure of all the fullness of God" (Eph. 3:19), we should recognize and embrace them for precisely what they are: opportunities to experience His fullness!

Consequently, every time we see James, the son of Alphaeus' name among the disciples who made the Providential cut, an opportunity exists for us to trust God for being both divinely beautiful and mysterious. Making the most of that opportunity by choosing to believe our Lord when we can't wholly unmask Him will strengthen our faith, not weaken it.

EMBRACING PARADOX

A paradox is a seemingly absurd or self-contradictory statement that *may* be well-founded or true upon further investigation. They are quite common in literary masterpieces. Consider these:

"I can resist everything except temptation."[109]

"I must be cruel to be kind."[110]

"Death, thou shalt die."[111]

Be not surprised, therefore, that in the most celebrated literary masterpiece in human history, James, the son of Alphaeus, holds a place within the list of Jesus' disciples that should count as ample evidence that biblical paradoxes do indeed exist.

And he's just one of many paradoxes in the New Testament. Consider these, for example:

> "Anyone who loves their life will lose it, while anyone who hates their life in this world will keep it for eternal life" (John 12:25).

> "You have been set free from sin and have become slaves to righteousness" (Rom. 6:18).

> "That is why, for Christ's sake, I delight in weaknesses, in insults, in hardships, in persecutions, in difficulties. For when I am weak, then I am strong" (2 Cor. 12:10).

> "What is more, I consider everything a loss compared to the surpassing worth of knowing Christ Jesus my Lord, for whose sake I have lost all things. I consider them garbage, that I may gain Christ" (Phil. 3:8).

> "Humble yourselves before the Lord, and he will lift you up" (James 4:10).

Unlike these, the one that is this James is unique because his name itself is paradoxical. Mark's assigning James, the son of Alphaeus, as *tou mikrou* probably means James, the son of Zebedee, had a few years on him. It also more than likely implies that his influence was less than the other disciple with the same name.

We Westerners have a problem with the concept of a paradox because much of the rationalism in our culture originated from Aristotle's Law of Non-Contradiction. He argued that two things could not be true at the same time and in the same relationship.[112] In most cases, that's true. Either the sky is blue today, or it's not. Jesus is "the Way, the Truth, and the Life," or He's not.

Biblical paradoxes, however, force us to think through why we believe the way we do. They are spiritual principles that are true at the same time and in the same relationship, even though they appear contradictory.

Consider, for example, the two-thousand-year-old debate between God's election and man's free will. When people lure me into this conversation, I respond that we have the capacity and ability to choose whether or not to obey. That is free will, and it is biblical. God, however, has free will, too. And it most certainly trumps ours. That is the election of saints by Divine choice, which is equally biblical.

Writers of the Scriptures saw no issue juxtaposing both concepts and holding them in tension. We shouldn't have problems with paradoxes either; neither should we fight about them. Let's embrace them instead. Worship and praise God for them when we run across one, just like we do when we sing about the Trinity.

AN ILLUSTRATION OF GOD'S CAPACITY TO CHANGE PEOPLE

Jesus also included James, the son of Alphaeus, in His league to show us that He is in the business of changing people's lives. The name Alphaeus means "changing."[113] What an image! God's story in the lives of every single one of the disciples whose name was not Judas Iscariot was that they needed radical transformation that only He could orchestrate. The same story applies to us. God will recast us into what He wants us to be as we walk with Him.

He took an impulsive denier like Peter and turned him into immovable limestone. He sculpted the Sons of Thunder into vessels of mercy. And, friends, Jesus chose James, the son of Alphaeus, because He was going to use him to usher in the New Covenant and change the way we approach God.

The veil in the Holy of Holies was torn on the Friday that Christ died. When Jesus arose, His work was complete. As a result, we no longer need to go to a high priest and confess our sins to receive satisfactory atonement and forgiving mercy. We can go to Him directly. Jesus unveiled the face of God the Father and made access to Him possible through Calvary when He sprang to life again inside Joseph of Arimathea's tomb.

ABOUT THAT UNKNOWN TOMB

By the way, advances in mitochondrial DNA testing helped scientists determine on May 14, 1998, that one of the previously unknown soldiers in the tomb was Air Force 1st Lieutenant Michael Joseph Blassie.[114] When God chose to reveal this lieutenant in his full heroic glory, our Lord let us know about it.

This James could very well be the half-brother of Jesus and the writer of the Book of James. He could also be Matthew's brother; he could even be an ordinary guy named James, whose father was a regular guy named Alphaeus. If and when God wants to make him fully known to us, He certainly will.

Though we know only a little bit about him now, on that day when we see him in Heaven, we shall fully know this James as we are fully known (1 Cor. 13:12). That is because we entered the tent the same way both of Jesus' disciples named James did—with the faith of a child.

SOME QUESTIONS TO PONDER BEFORE MOVING ON

1. Read Isaiah 55:8-9. How might we rest in God's higher ways when we cannot make sense of His plan?

2. Read Matthew 16:24-26. What is the paradox? How has it impacted your life both negatively and positively?

3. Read 1 Timothy 6:6. How might jealousy of someone else rob of us contentment? In what ways has your love for Christ and comfort in Him added value to unfavorable circumstances?

Chapter 12

THE JUDAS ISCARIOT DISGUISE

OF ALL THE UNPLEASANT THINGS in life, lizards and beets share the top prize in my world for the Worst Things on the Planet. I prefer sleeping on a chicken-wire mattress to eating a beet, especially when they are boiled and start bleeding right there in the pot.

And, friend, if I see a lizard, I'm running. I started that habit in childhood when my next-door neighbor's pet *chamaeleoninae*[115]—which you know as a chameleon—snuck up on me and started hissing and flashing his colors while I was playing a video game. The sprinting skills I developed when I encountered Mr. Charlie Change Colors on that day are still intact. We have no plans on meeting anytime soon to repair our severed relationship either.

I've read enough about chameleons from a distance, however, to know that they are astute and resourceful reptiles. They're not hot-headed or impulsive like Peter was. If they could speak to their fellow reptilian brethren, they would listen and observe before they uttered a single word. That's because chameleons have the rarest of eyes—eyes that can see with a 360-degree arc of vision completely around their bodies. Such a trait makes them quite perceptive.

They can also change colors to regulate their body temperature to protect themselves from danger. Such a quality helps them adapt to their environment and aids them greatly in their survival. If chameleons took on human form and got a job leading an organization, they would think through tough decisions long before making them. They might also make connections with movers and shakers at the highest levels of influence to ensure their organization has the necessary influential and transformative push to make it successful.

And I assure you they would insist on handling the company's loot because they are quite resourceful with their, well, resources. Feed a chameleon an insect for a day, and he's happy. If not, he'll eat a leaf and still be satisfied. They certainly know how to live and use what's available to keep them functioning until another opportunity comes along.

In great literary masterpieces, an antagonist often comes and changes colors to try to spoil the goal of the protagonist. Their attempts to do this require resourcefulness and perceptiveness, just like a chameleon. Professor Moriarity changed his colors quite frequently in his efforts to thwart Sherlock Holmes' investigations.[116] Claudius did, too, when he seized the throne and married Gertrude while Prince Hamlet was away at school.[117]

The New Testament isn't just a literary masterpiece, nor is it a work of fiction; it's the non-fictional story of how God became flesh and dwelt among us to restore humanity to Himself through the cross at a particular time in history. Jesus is the Protagonist of the story. And the devil is the antagonist. He mobilized Judas Iscariot to take on the qualities of a chameleon and adapt to his environment just so he could thwart the redemptive goal of God.

Judas Iscariot disguised himself as good to be effective in his influence. On the outside, Judas appeared righteous and pious. Beneath the surface, however, lay a resourceful imposter who serves as the clearest biblical explanation of how Satan himself operates within the highest spheres of Christian influence to seduce the masses and thwart Provident plans.

WHY JUDAS

Biblical writers often contrasted different physical realities—light and darkness, for example—to teach spiritual truths. Isaiah was particularly good at this, writing, "The people walking in darkness have seen a great light; on those living in the land of deep darkness a light has dawned" (Isa. 9:2).

John wasn't too bad at it either: "God is light; in him there is no darkness at all. If we claim to have fellowship with him and yet walk in darkness, we lie and do not live out the truth. But if we walk in the light, as he is in the light, we have fellowship with one another, and the blood of Jesus, his Son, purifies us from all sin" (1 John 1:5-7).

And the apostle Paul excelled in the contrast department, too: "For God, who said, 'Let light shine out of darkness,' made his light shine in our hearts to give us the light of the knowledge of God's glory displayed in the face of Christ" (2 Cor. 4:6).

Light is sacred in the Bible because it represents God in His purest essence. Since He created it (Gen. 1:3) and is clothed in it (Psalm 104:2), how could it not? On the other hand, darkness represents the domain where sacredness and holiness do not exist. It's the realm of Satan, where there is not only an absence of light, but also "weeping and the gnashing of teeth" (Matt. 22:13).

So, from a thematic narrative standpoint, Jesus, the protagonist of the New Testament Gospels, is the light and very representation of God for the world. I doubt you're surprised. On the other hand, Judas, the antagonist, is the exact opposite; he's the very representation of Satanic evil and how it works.

The contrast is significant because it implies the character of God and the Evil One are on full display within the story of the disciples. If it's possible to learn the essence of sacredness and what is for us the highest good by studying Jesus' disciples, then the opposite is also true. It is possible to learn what the God Who inspired the New Testament considers egregious evil by reflecting on the life of Judas Iscariot. To unmask him is to bare the face and character of Satan himself and how he operates in the world, especially within the circles of God's people.

WHO HE WAS

A BLENDING CHAMELEON

Like a chameleon, Judas blended in well with truth-seeking followers of Jesus. As a result, he hoodwinked people into thinking he cared about what they did: pleasing their Master by studying His character and then trying to emulate it. Instead, he was his own master, one who was hostile to the truth and certainly had no intention of applying it to his own life. Instead of hiding the Word of God in his heart in anticipation of the work that laid ahead for the disciples after the ascension, Judas could only hiss and change colors.

The name Judas was common in the first century. So common that Jesus called another disciple to Himself with the same name (Luke 6:16). Luke also mentions a Galilean man named Judas in his account of Gamliel's speech to the Sanhedrin in the book of Acts (5:37). It comes from the Hebrew word *yada*, meaning "to praise."[118] As a result, to separate him from those of nobler character with the same name, the Gospel writers designate him as *Judas Iscariot*.

His last name means "man of Kerioth," denoting the small town in southern Judea where he lived.[119] What's important to note, however, is that town's name comes from the Hebrew word *kara*, which denotes the ideas of planning with others to subject someone or something to disaster.[120] Such an activity came naturally to Judas. It was in his blood.

God's name never changes in the Scriptures. He is the same yesterday, today, and forevermore (Heb. 13:8). But people's names do change quite often within the sacred pages, most especially after a transformative spiritual encounter of some kind.

Abram had one; God changed his name to Abraham after it (Gen. 17:5). Jacob did, too, which is why God changed his name to Israel (Gen. 32:28). And most importantly for our subject, Simon became Peter after confessing that Jesus was the Christ (Matt. 16:18).

But Judas Iscariot's name does not change in the Scriptures because he never had a transformative spiritual encounter with the God of the Bible. As his first name suggests, he praised Jesus around others. But as his last name suggests, his heart was hell-bent on conspiring against the Lord to cause considerable harm. As William Shakespeare said, "To say the truth, Judas kiss'd his master, and cried 'all hail!' when as he meant all harm."[121]

Such treasonous behavior came naturally to Judas. And God knew him for who he was: a chameleon who conspires and plots harm, just like Satan.

The point is this: Judas surrounded himself by truth but never applied it. He was present for the miracles of Christ, but they meant nothing to him. He walked and talked with redeemed pariahs like Matthew and Simon the Zealot, but the grace extended to them failed to register in his carnal mind. Judas lacked interest in the substance of the message in the first place.

In that sense, he was a lot like Gehazi of 2 Kings 5. He witnessed his master, Elisha, heal the Syrian Naaman of leprosy and reject a love offering because of it. After he left Elisha's presence, though, Gehazi chased Naaman down and exploited him for his financial gain. He never applied truth in his life, either. Outwardly, they both appeared righteous, outstanding, moral people. Inwardly, however, they were hostile in mind and conspired in their hearts to commit evil deeds (Col. 1:21).

Both inherited this malady from Satan. As an angel, he resided in glory. He saw it personally but never experienced it. The thought of existing under perfect holiness, glory, and benevolence horrified him because he was inwardly hostile.

Satan was so incredulous to righteousness that he had schemed to be close to Divine beauty, majesty, and benevolence so that he could usurp God Himself. What he really wanted to do in Heaven was shape God's angels into his image. That's why he led a rebellion in God's abode (Job 4:18). He failed; Judas did, too. That's why Luke makes sure to tell us that he killed himself (Acts 1:18) and went to where he belonged: ever present with his mentor and example in hell.

HIGHLY AMBITIOUS

John tells us (John 12:6) that Judas was the "keeper of the money bag" and stole from it—from the ministry of the New Covenant, mind you—because he was a thief. He also had very high religious connections. Luke writes, "Judas went to the chief priests and the officers of the temple guard and discussed with them how he might betray Jesus" (Luke 22:4).

In the time of the New Testament, an internal civil war between the Jews was going on because of how chief priests rose to power. It started when two individuals by the name of Aristobulus and Hyrcanus both laid claim to the high priesthood and looked to the Roman official Pompey to solve it during last century before the ministry of John the Baptist.[122]

The internal struggle for control of religion meant that the priests dispatched guards to watch over the sanctuaries for fear of a coup d'état, thus the reason for John's reference to the "detachment of soldiers and officials from the chief priests" who accompanied Judas to the Garden of Gethsemane in his sojourn of betrayal carrying "torches, lanterns and weapons" (John 18:3). Unless they knew you, you weren't entering to inform them of anything. But they knew Judas; he had the right connections. Add the love of money with ambition and deception, and you have a recipe for pure evil.

History is replete with examples of highly ambitious individuals who opportunistically buddied up to movers and shakers because they needed wealth and power to carry out their agenda for the world. The Right Reverend Grigori Rasputin, for example, befriended Russian Tsar Nicholas II because he wanted to shape Russia's political course.[123] He also buddied up to his wife for the same reason, thereby making the nation a laughingstock among her enemies because of it.

James, John, and their mother, Salome, tried. Judas did, too. But what separated the former from the latter was their response to Jesus' rebuke. The Thunder Brothers and their mother accepted it and became wise. Judas and Rasputin did the opposite and became fools. Jesus uttered correctional words encased in love to heal him (Prov. 27:6). Judas, however, chose profuse kisses in the Garden of Gethsemane to show his utter contempt and disdain instead.

Satan works in and through individuals who worship power, wealth, and fame. He especially delights in those who care the most about how they are perceived, especially in religious arenas. He must disguise himself in such a way to be effective. But when that evil disguise is unveiled and rebuked for precisely what it is, the response is more often than not a narcissistic rage for someone who wears Judas' skin.

Don't be deceived. Everyone on this Earth belongs to one kingdom or the other. There is no such thing as middle spirituality in the economy of the Kingdom of God. There is only lost or found, sheep or goat. All people will carry out God's purposes, regardless of how they act. But how people behave, most especially in Christian settings, will determine whether they carry out His Provident purposes like Zebedee's family, or like Judas.

ABLE TO LEAD AND INFLUENCE

This infamous disciple could also lead and influence people. John saw this firsthand, narrating:

> Then Mary took about a pint of pure nard, an expensive perfume; she poured it on Jesus' feet and wiped his feet with her hair. And the house was filled with the fragrance of the perfume. But one of his disciples, Judas Iscariot, who was later to betray him, objected, 'Why wasn't this perfume sold and the money given to the poor? It was worth a year's wages.' He did not say this because he cared about the poor but because he was a thief; as keeper of the money bag, he used to help himself to what was put into it (John 12:3-6).

Judas objected to Mary's (Lazarus' sister) expression of worshipping Jesus that involved the pouring of expensive perfume on his feet because they could've sold it and given the money to the poor. Judas, however, was not concerned in any way whatsoever with the poor. He was only worried about the fact that the perfume was expensive because he wanted to profit from it. So, he spoke up because he wished the jar to swell. What he didn't want to do was to be forthright and honest about his motives. For such openness would have revealed who he was at his core.

His question is seemingly noble on the surface. It's not, though; Judas asked it to draw the disciples' attention away from Jesus. That's what someone wearing Judas' skin does: turns the attention of Christ-followers away from Jesus and onto something else that isn't bad in and of itself. Because when the wolf in sheep's clothing applies such tactics, he becomes the master, not Christ.

This soldier of the devil had to appear loving. That's what made him effective. Such an effort explains why all the disciples not named Judas Iscariot had no clue who would betray Jesus. Peter, bless his soul, thought it was him because he nudged John and quipped, "Ask him which one he means" (John 13:24).

John obliged, which implies that even he did not know! Had Judas dropped the disguise, he would have surrendered his influence. He was too proud to do that. He was much more comfortable in his malevolent skin, saying: "Surely you don't mean me, Lord?" (Matt. 26:22).

Judas knew the answer to that question; he just didn't want the rest of the disciples to know he did! He feared exposure for who he was more than anything: an anti-Christ who was more comfortable hijacking the Garden of Eden with the serpent than following Jesus.

A DECEITFUL DOUBTER

Judas was also a deceitful doubter. Satan is, too. Many well-intentioned ministers of the Gospel council their flocks with statements like "never doubt." Heroes of the Scriptures, however, had plenty of them.

Habakkuk did: "How long, Lord, must I call for help, but you do not listen?" (1:2).

So did David: "My God, my God, why have you forsaken me? Why are you so far from saving me, so far from my cries of anguish? My God, I cry out by day, but you do not answer, by night, but I find no rest" (Psalm 22:1-2).

John the Baptist wasn't exempt from doubting God either: "Are you the one who is to come, or should we expect someone else?" (Matt. 11:3).

All of these men asked God honest questions and continued to trust Him when the Almighty didn't answer them. To doubt, in essence, is to be human, especially as it pertains to the issue of good versus evil. Honest doubt can strengthen faith on the other side of it, as was the case with Thomas.

Judas' doubt was different. Dishonesty and deception rode in the passenger seat of his skeptical Cadillac. He doubted Jesus because he had a problem with God. Witnessing more miracles or hearing more theological discourses would not have sustained Judas or sufficiently answered his questions. He was never concerned with what was truthful in the first place.

A HATER OF CORRECTION

Unlike the rest of the disciples, Judas hated correction. Satan does, too. All disciples not named Judas experienced the chastisement of the Lord and humbled themselves in light of it. Peter, for example, faced the reality of his sinfulness when Jesus rebuked him over and over. He learned from it and grew stronger because he knew love guided the sacred discipline.

When rebuked by Jesus, Peter could face his shadow and confront the imposter within.[124] John and James could, too, but Judas could not. When Jesus rebuked him, the imposter within raged against him and made him hostile to the point that he was eager and willing to betray Him for a couple of bucks.

HIS LESSON FOR US

The Gospel writers mention Judas' betrayal of Jesus, not just because they are concerned with telling us how the good triumphs over evil. They also include him to warn us that "those who fail to learn from history are doomed to repeat its errors."[125] Evil is real; it's among God's people every day in the highest places of Christian leadership and influence.

Paul told the church at Ephesus, "For our struggle is not against flesh and blood, but against the rulers, against the authorities, against the powers of this dark world and against the spiritual forces of evil in the heavenly realms" (Eph. 6:12).

Regardless of the Christian endeavor, this will be true from now until the end of time. Genuine humility before God that's demonstrated by love for Him and neighbor is the hallmark of Christian righteousness, not narcissistic rage that inspires malicious deeds. Such an explosion is a fruit of the flesh.

Should that flesh pattern continue throughout a person's life without ever surrendering it to Christ, then that individual has chosen to be clothed in the skin of Judas—not the righteousness of Christ—regardless of how they are perceived. Because behind the religious disguise is a person who loves darkness more than light (John 3:19), just like Satan.

SOME QUESTIONS TO PONDER BEFORE MOVING ON

1. Read Genesis 3:1 and Ecclesiastes 1:9. How does doubting what God has spoken manifest itself in our world today? In what ways has it materialized in your life? What lesson was God trying to teach you?

2. Read Habakkuk 1:3-4, 12-17 and 3:17-18. What does Habakkuk do with his doubts at the end of the book? In what ways can you trust God through your misgivings?

3. Read Matthew 27:3-4 and Luke 19:1-10. What's the difference between remorse and repentance? Which approach to our sin determines our eternal destiny?

Chapter 13

JUDAS, NOT ISCARIOT: THE DISCIPLE WITH ONE LINE

I BROKE MY FINGER AS a lad falling out of a tree in my grandfather's yard. Like me, he knew I had to go to the emergency room. But also like me, he loathed the waiting part that goes with it. Fortunately, though, he had connections to a doctor friend and gave him a buzz to see if he could fit me into his schedule. He could, so we made a beeline for his office.

Upon arrival, we simultaneously noticed a sign that read *The Medical Practice of I Don't Remember the Fella's Name*. Always the king of timely one-liners, my grandfather quipped, "Derrick, why do medical doctors refer to what they do as 'practice'?" I understood at that moment why my grandmother got irritated at the manifestation of his sense of humor at the most inopportune times.

One-liners are part of our cultural jargon because they are usually easy to remember. We can also use them to get laughs. The entrepreneurs among us might even start a bumper sticker business off them.

Consider this one I saw a couple of weeks ago: "Treat each day as your last; one day you will be right."

I would question your taste in movies if you are not familiar with these one-liners: "E.T. phone home."[126] "Yo, Adrian."[127] "May the force be with you."[128]

I can think of many great one-liners in the Bible, too. My favorite is "Better to live on a corner of the roof than share a house with a quarrelsome wife" (Prov. 25:24). On the other hand, my wife has this verse on the tip of her tongue when I spout out mine: "But Jael, Heber's wife, picked up a tent peg and a hammer and went quietly to him while he lay fast asleep" (Judg. 4:21). I usually concede the theological debate at that point.

There once was a Judas who walked with Jesus who wasn't evil. As a matter of fact, to separate him from the one who was, John calls him *Judas Not Iscariot*. Out of the 3,779 verses in the New Testament Gospels, this mysterious Judas plays an active role in just one of them. It's in the form of a question: "Then Judas (not Judas Iscariot) said, 'But, Lord, why do you intend to show yourself to us and not to the world?'" (John 14:22).

Jesus answered his question in fifty-one verses, the most extensive answer to any query in the New Testament. That's right; to Judas Not Iscariot goes the title of *The Best Biblical Question Asker*. Do you think that makes him valuable? Yes, I do, too.

THE TRINOMINOUS DISCIPLE

Trinominous? That's a big word, Derrick! Yep, and it contains two Latin root words: "tri" (three) and "nomos" (name). Jerome, the early fourth-century church father, used it to describe this Judas.[129] His information helps us understand a little bit about who he was and clear up any peripheral discrepancies about him.

Luke refers to him as Judas, the Son of James (Luke 6:16). In the original language of the New Testament, Matthew calls him Lebbaeus and then tells us his "surname was Thaddaeus." And in several old Latin manuscripts of Matthew's Gospel, he's deemed Judas Zelotes, or Judas the Zealot.[130] Only Mark references him as Thaddaeus (Mark 3:18). I love that name because it denotes the ideas of "sweetness" and "gentleness of character."[131]

Read together with the form of his question, we can reasonably postulate that Judas Lebbaeus Thaddaeus was a Zealot in political outlook but not in personality. He wanted the Romans out of his land as much as Simon; he was better killing the Romans with kindness than his friend, though. Thus, the reason he wanted to know why Jesus, the Messiah, seemed only interested in making Himself known just to His disciples and not to the world.

Judas Lebbaeus Thaddaeus wanted a Jewish monarch who would banish Israel's enemies by force. A Messiah Who physically suffered for the sins of their enemies to save them was inconceivable to him.[132] So Jesus took the opportunity to educate all of the disciples on a fundamental lesson often missed: "The way of power can never be substituted for the way of love."[133] What Judas Not Iscariot didn't know at the time was that Jesus was going to use His gentle spirit—a trait reflected by the way he tactfully asked the question—to make himself known to the world!

A PROVIDENTIAL DISSERTATION

I have the vexatious gift of answering a question with a question. It gets under people's skin, primarily when I engage in conversations like this one:

"Hey, Derrick, why do you take the Bible seriously?"

"Do you take the Bible seriously?"

"No."

"Then why do you want me to answer your question seriously?"

Jesus, however, is much different from me. He often followed up questions from His inquisitors with rebuttal queries. Such an approach called attention to spiritual issues they had not adequately addressed in their lives. The rich, young ruler, for example, asked Him: "Good teacher, what must I do to inherit eternal life?" (Luke 18:18). To which Jesus thought-provokingly countered, "Why do you call me good?" (Luke 18:19).

But Jesus did no such thing when Judas Lebbaeus Thaddaeus asked his question. Instead, He responded clearly and gave him a providential dissertation on the person and work of the Holy Spirit and how they all should relate to Him.

THE SPIRIT INDWELLS

Just before this disciple's question, Jesus had already alluded to the third Person of the God-head when He told them all: "The world cannot accept him, because it neither sees him nor knows him. But you know him, for he lives with you and will be in you" (John 14:17). The reason He did was simple. Every person in the world is the son or daughter of Adam, with the judgment of sin stamped into his or her soul (Rom. 5:12). But the work of their Teacher on the cross that soon followed this conversation made their redemption possible. Because of the work of the second Adam—the One speaking to them (Rom. 5:15)—they would learn to operate in and through the power of God's Spirit. That's something unregenerate people in the world cannot do.

Such a lesson prompted Judas Not Iscariot to ask the question. Jesus then used His inquest as a launching pad, going into even more detail. He told them all that the reason He let them see His omnipotence through the miraculous was so that they, His followers, would make disciples in it. And such an endeavor could only be accomplished through the power and work of the Holy Spirit. He did not perform miracles so they would say, "Wow. What an awesome magic show!" Jesus performed them so they would "stand amazed in the presence of Jesus the Nazarene" and sing, "How marvelous and wonderful is my Savior's love for me."[134]

Our Lord knew if he led them to the College of the Bent Knee by revealing Himself through miracles, they would place their faith in Him and make disciples of other rebels as "far as the curse is found."[135] Their assignment after His ascension was to call others to join the rebel's choir. And for such a task, the disciples would need Divine help. That's why Jesus' answer to him was a detailed explanation of the role and work of the third Person of the Trinity, the Holy Spirit.

Think about the implications of the indwelling of the Spirit of God for a moment. It implies we are never alone in this world; we aren't orphans (John 14:18). Jesus' Spirit resides permanently inside of us. Our Lord told Judas Not

Iscariot as much: "Anyone who loves me will obey my teaching. My Father will love them, and we will come to them and make our home with them" (John 14:23).

The last phrase alludes to the tabernacle of Exodus fame (Exod. 25:1-9). This portable structure housed God's presence while the Israelites sojourned to the Promised Land. The Jewish temple's Holy of Holies became that place of God's dwelling while the Israelites resided in the land.

John, however, tells us something even more important about God's presence: "The Word became flesh and <u>made his dwelling among us.</u> We have seen his glory, the glory of the one and only Son, who came from the Father, full of grace and truth" (John 1:14—emphasis mine).

Did you catch the progression? The presence of God has now moved from two buildings—one portable and one fixed—to a person: Jesus. And continuing the progression, our Lord tells Judas Not Iscariot and the rest of the disciples that they are now that place of God's residence. By faith, love, and obedience—all of which denote an authentic relationship with the God of the Bible—the disciples would have an opportunity to play a part in one of the Bible's great themes: God's Presence Among Us.

What an answer to this disciple's question! Jesus wasn't even close to finishing His message and giving the altar call either. He was just getting started.

THE SPIRIT TEACHES AND GLORIFIES HIS SON

When I get to Heaven, I'm going to ask this Judas if he had any earthly idea that his question would elicit such a detailed response from Jesus about how the Spirit works. I doubt he did.

Jesus continued, telling Judas Lebbaeus Thaddaeus within an earshot of the other disciples that the Spirit of God will remind them of everything He taught them (John 14:26); help them fulfill their mission to make disciples (John 14:17); and serve as their Counselor, Advocate, Comforter, and Intercessor (John 14:26).

THE SPIRIT ENABLES CONNECTION TO THE SON

Judas and his friends had a steep road ahead, but so did Jesus. So, He assured him with an instructive lesson about vines and the fruit they produce. Both were essential images for understanding Jesus' message, and He used them frequently in His conversations with the disciples.[136] In the Old Testament, vines and vineyards are synonymous with the people of God, the planter and cultivator of them with God Himself.[137]

But in this response to Judas' question, Jesus flips the script, calling Himself the Vine—not Israel, Judas, or the rest of the disciples (John 15:1, 5). He was and still is the embodiment of what Israel was meant to be but was not.[138] Judas, and the others, would have picked up on that. That's why what follows was imperative for them to understand: "If you remain in me and I in you, you will bear much fruit; apart from me you can do nothing" (John 15:5).

Without abiding in the presence of God, Judas and the rest of the disciples were not capable of bearing the fruit Jesus desired them to produce. How, then, were they to abide? He tells them: "If you remain in me and my words remain in you, <u>ask whatever you wish</u>, and it will be done for you" (John 15:7—emphasis mine).

Jesus' instruction here is conditional. "If" the disciples think about what Jesus stands for and pray in light of it, God will answer their prayers. That's the essence of abiding in Christ. Since Jesus is merciful, they can pray for God to help them show it to others and be sure God will grant their request. They can pray for joy in difficult circumstances and be sure Jesus will hear and answer that request also.

But Judas Not Iscariot and his friends can equally be sure that if they forget what Jesus stands for, God will not respond to their petitions. That's part of the condition. Abiding in Christ, then, implies praying in view of His character, something they would have to do to be successful in what God had for them to do in the near future. The same is true for us.

DOES THAT ANSWER YOUR QUESTION, JUDAS?

Jesus gave Judas Not Iscariot quite the answer to his question. He essentially told him, "The precise reason I've chosen to reveal Myself to you and not the world is that I have made you a new person—a new creature in Christ—and I will guide you as you operate in My Spirit to make disciples that love Me and love people in the world."

Jesus became what Israel was supposed to be: a light to the nations. Isaiah prophesied this: "I will also make you a light for the Gentiles, that my salvation may reach to the ends of the earth" (Isa. 49:6).

Now Judas and his friends would fulfill the same role every time they shared the Gospel through the power of the Holy Spirit. What a revelation! What a fantastic legacy for the disciple with one line, whose question is sealed within the sacred pages of John's Gospel forever!

While he may play a minor role in the New Testament in terms of volume, Judas Not Iscariot's significance isn't minuscule. His question not only revealed his love and devotion to Christ; it also gave Jesus the launching pad He needed for unveiling the best material on the Holy Spirit's role in our lives in all of the Bible.

My friends, the reason Jesus calls us into the tent is because He demands our hearts be ruled unconditionally by the power and work of His Spirit. To do that, He has to pardon us first by grace through faith alone. Then, our Lord empowers us by His Spirit so that we can show His pardoning and merciful character to the world. And it is demonstrated and proclaimed triumphantly when the Divine ethos of loving God and neighbor is evident in our lives. That was God's plan for the world when Judas asked the question two thousand years ago. It is the Almighty's plan now and will be His plan until He comes again.

SOME QUESTIONS TO PONDER BEFORE MOVING ON

1. Read John 14:25-26. In what ways does the Holy Spirit "help" you in the following areas: (1) Bible study (2) Decision-making (3) Discernment?

2. Read John 14:27-31 and 15:18-25. Biblical peace isn't the absence of conflict. Instead, it is the continual presence of God, even amid great personal strife. What are some areas of personal conflict in your life where you need the Holy Spirit to apply that definition?

3. Read John 16:5-10, 15. What are the essential roles of the Holy Spirit in people's lives who do not have a relationship with Jesus? What is the critical role of the Holy Spirit in a follower of Jesus' life according to verse fifteen?

Conclusion

SIX HONEST-SERVING MEN: WHAT, WHY, WHEN, HOW, WHERE, AND WHO

MY PARENTS GAVE ME THE Inquisitive Child label at an early age for a good reason. Bombarding them with questions—all kinds of them—came as naturally to me as breathing. I still vividly remember this infamous interrogation of my mother while she washed dishes: "Why do the folks who make lemon juice use artificial flavoring, while those who manufacture dishwashing liquid use real lemons?"

Though I didn't get special brownies for my queries at home, my investigative approach to life served me quite well in my educational endeavors. I learned it from Rudyard Kipling: "I keep six honest serving-men, they taught me all I knew; their names are what and why and when and how and where and who."[139]

These honest men provide the proper framework for correctly interpreting the Bible—one based on the uninterrupted covenantal flow within its sacred pages—and aid us mightily in understanding exactly how Jesus' calling of the Twelve impacts you and me. Neither can be learned by osmosis or by observing the Lion King from the parade route.

Like the disciples, you have to start with the free ticket God left for you at the cross outside the tent two thousand years ago. It has no expiration date; it's still dripping with the blood, sweat, tears, anguish, justice, grace, and mercy our Lord Jesus showed us. For the quest to understand His character, as well as our relationship with Him, as revealed in His Holy Book stops and starts with a straightforward principle: unmerited favor. Of that, I am convinced. By now, you should be also.

WHAT THE MESSAGE OF THE ORIGINAL TWELVE MEANS FOR US NOW

Remember that chapter at the beginning about mountains? I didn't write it to take up space. Without understanding the concept of biblical mountains as places where God speaks, we won't connect the commission of the Twelve to ours.

Regardless of whether they believed in Jesus as their Messiah or rejected Him as such, Jews reading the Gospels for the very first time would have immediately understood the implications of what Matthew, Mark, Luke, and John were trying to say about Jesus' mission. They knew these writings were a polemic for a new Divine government under the sole leadership of Jesus the Christ. Some chose to languish in their unbelief; others trusted what they said about the Messiah.

The writer of Hebrews belongs in the latter category, stating, "You have not come to a mountain that can be touched and that is burning with fire; to darkness, gloom and storm; to a trumpet blast or to such a voice speaking words that those who heard it begged that no further word be spoken to them" (Heb. 12:18-19). That mountain they—followers of Jesus—have not come to is Mount Sinai of Mosaic fame. After receiving the Law from God there (Exod. 20-31), Moses descended and stumbled upon the Israelites passing the time by worshipping a golden calf at the base of the mountain (Exod. 32:1-34). When the Lord sent a plague as punishment (Exod. 32:35), they got spooked and wanted no more of this exclusive worship of the God of Israel thing.

Now, think about that for just a moment. How many times have you heard some well-intentioned individual mutter something utterly foolish along the lines of, "All you have to do to be right before God is to just follow the Ten Commandments?"

The problem with such a statement is that those commands were never designed to save. They can only condemn because they show us what sin against God looks like in our lives (Rom. 3:19-20). Without Jesus, we will eternally fellowship with the Israelites at the base of the mountain by impaling ourselves on the horns of the sacred cows we construct in our image.

Thus, the writer of Hebrews continues:

> But you have come to Mount Zion, to the city of the living God, the heavenly Jerusalem. You have come to thousands upon thousands of angels in joyful assembly, to the church of the firstborn, whose names are written in heaven. You have come to God, the Judge of all, to the spirits of the righteous made perfect, to Jesus the mediator of a new covenant, and to the sprinkled blood that speaks a better word than the blood of Abel" (Heb. 12:22-24).

See that word "mediator"? It evokes the idea of someone who inserts himself into the middle of a conflict to bring resolution. Before Jesus called the Twelve, they were hostile in mind toward God and engaged in evil deeds (Col. 1:21). So were we. But instead of smiting us with a plague, which we deserve, God the Father penalized His Son on the cross with the scourge of our wickedness.

That's what discipleship meant for the disciples then, and that's what it means for us today. Your best effort will not get you inside the tent of the Promised Land, my friend. Just ask Moses. You must enter via the cross and only the cross. After you do, don't use old wineskins in your approach to fellowshipping with Him either. Live in the right covenant—the one on the right side of the cross elucidated in the second half of the Good Book. The disciples were commissioned to proclaim that message in their world, and they did. It's the message we've been authorized to declare in ours, and we shall.

WHEN AND WHERE JESUS CHOSE THIS METHOD TO INSTITUTE A NEW COVENANT

You might be tempted to say, "Hey, preacher man, I know the when and where. It happened two thousand years ago when Jesus called the disciples in the region of Galilee and died on a cross in Jerusalem."

Nope. It transpired before the world began. Before brussel sprouts, fig trees, Mickey Mouse, and you and me, the Triune God hatched a glorious plan to restore humanity to Himself and implemented it while seated on His eternal throne.

In the Parable of Wheat and Tares, Jesus explained to His disciples that He was commissioned by His father to announce something hidden since the foundation of the world: the Kingdom of God (Matt. 13:35). Though unknown to the Old Testament greats, this League of Pardoned Rebels would know it fully by walking with Jesus, witnessing His ascension, and relying on the Holy Spirit in their lives after the Lord returned to His eternal abode. On that wise trail, Jesus taught them the following:

1. Faith comes by hearing and responding to the message of the New Covenant in a way that spiritually reproduces (Matt. 13:1-9).

2. The Kingdom of God starts very small, like a mustard seed. Over time, it becomes a hulking tree inside the soul that's able to provide comfort, shade, and rest for the creatures of the garden (Matt. 13:31-33).

3. The essence of that kingdom message is radical forgiveness, regardless of the offense (Matt. 18:21-35).

4. And proof that their faith germinated from good soil was going to be demonstrated most clearly in how they went about loving the least of these (Matt. 25:31-46).

Since this was Jesus' planned message of restoration He instituted before the foundation of the world, dare we suggest another? It's not a plan of condemnation or counting trespasses; it's one of Divine mercy that leads to freedom, joy, and a love for people. That was the world-changing message they were commissioned to proclaim, and they did. Just ask Matthew. And they passed the baton forward through time right into our hands. So, as we run the race of discipleship, may we never forget to hand it off to others.

WHOM JESUS USES AND HOW HE USES THEM

I have no clue who wrote this poem because it is anonymous. I suspect, however, that the person who did was close to someone in the ministry:

When God wants to drill a man,
And thrill a man,
And skill a man.
When God wants to mold a man
To play the noblest part;

When He yearns with all His heart
To create so great and bold a man,
That all the world shall be amazed,
Watch His methods, watch His ways!

How He ruthlessly perfects
Whom He royally elects!
How He hammers him and hurts him,
And with mighty blows converts him;

Into trial shapes of clay which
Only God understands;
While his tortured heart is crying
And he lifts beseeching hands!

How He bends but never breaks
When his good He undertakes;
How He uses whom He chooses,
And which every purpose fuses him;
By every act induces him
To try His splendor out—
God knows what He's about.[140]

It also describes how Jesus used the disciples to institute the New Covenant.

SIMON PETER

Have you ever been so convinced you were right about something only to find out you had no clue of that which you spoke? How many times have you said or done things you can't take back because your impulses—not Jesus—controlled you?

What about pledging allegiance to stand up for some noble cause in front of other like-minded people but cowering the moment you realized such a stand might negatively impact your wallet and social standing? Peter fell victim to those maladies; and apart from the unmerited favor of Christ, he, the coward, would have perished because of them. But he did not. He became a "bulwark never failing"[141] after the resurrection, faithful until his death upside down on a cruel Roman cross.[142]

THE SONS OF ZEBEDEE

Have you ever known bright individuals born into wealth and privilege who deceive themselves into thinking their social stature and material blessings qualify them to be an expert in theological issues and religious leadership? You've noticed some church folks operate like that, I'm sure. Put them together with business-savvy people who don't like being told no and ask them to wash the feet of the least of these. I dare you. Be ready for some pushback as their voices of thunder rage against you.

James and John, the sons of Zebedee, would agree, as would their mother. They were so privileged that Salome Zebedee wanted to earmark some family loot to fund Jesus' ministry if he decided to elevate her boys above the rest of the disciples. Qualifications or merit were immaterial. Status and money talked; humility and servanthood walked. Such behavior patterns demonstrate what being lost and dead in transgressions is all about.

Jesus, however, called them to Himself through unmerited favor. Consequently, they became different people. James left the family business and chose disgrace for the sake of Christ (Heb. 11:26)—greater worth than all of the Zebedee Fishing Company stock he was set to inherit. He paid for his Gospel-centeredness with his life, perishing by the sword of Herod Agrippa (Acts 12:1-2).

As for John, he proclaimed the Gospel in Ephesus well into his eighties.[143] He also wrote some pretty marvelous literary and theological masterpieces. Consider this one, for example: "In the beginning was the Word, and the Word was with God, and the Word was God" (John 1:1).

ANDREW AND JAMES, THE SON OF ALPHAEUS

The tent of Christ might have a narrow entry—as Peter, James, and John learned via public error and Provident correction—but it also has plenty of room inside for leaders who think and listen first and act second. I still suffer from "Foot in Mouth Disease" because I resort to impulsivity often in stressful situations. Andrew and Alphaeus' son had no such ailment.

Andrew suffered and died on a cross—like his Master—in Western Greece. But not before he took the Gospel to the Ukraine, Romania, and Russia, where he is considered a patron saint to this day.[144]

By one account, James, the son of Alphaeus, died at the age of ninety-four while preaching the Gospel in Jerusalem when an individual from the crowd hit him in the head with a fuller's club.[145] Another historical record assigns his missionary endeavors to Egypt, where he perished in Ostrakine courtesy of the same ancient weapon.[146] Both of these traditions have merit in terms of his Gospel work and fate given his portrayal with a fuller's club in some ancient Christian art.[147] Following his Lord's command (Matt. 28:18-20) and example, James, the son of Alphaeus, took the Gospel to a lost world and sealed his testimony in his blood.

NATHANAEL

Of all the mistakes I've made in ministry, looking down on others who were not as conversant in the Scriptures as I estimated myself to be is the one for which I am the most ashamed. The Gnostics, coined after a Greek word meaning "to know,"[148] were a group of heretics in the first and second centuries that applauded themselves for their intellectual and educational pedigree. That hubris, however, caused them to paint a picture of Jesus much different than the one in the New Testament.

Such a mentality in my life forced me to look in the mirror during a difficult time in ministry and make a painful conclusion. While I was orthodox in my theological outlook and, therefore, the exact opposite of a Gnostic in that regard (I still am), I was very much like them in the way I subconsciously looked down on others not as "well-versed" in theological issues as me.

Nathanael knew all about that. He had to learn from his Master that any intellectual endeavor to study and understand the Scriptures, however sincere, which manifests itself in a Gnostic attitude toward others is devoid of love. It is also Clanging Cymbal Christianity that blocks the doors of Heaven instead of trying to pry them open, which is one reason we study the Scriptures in the first place.

According to the late third and early fourth century church historian Eusebius, Nathanael took a copy of the Gospel of Matthew to India and left it there so they could experience the radical love of Christ the way he did.[149] We should follow his example wherever Christ leads.

MATTHEW

Speaking of mistakes, look no further than Matthew. I have no doubt he was chosen by Jesus on the mountain specifically because he wanted to show the world what He could do with an individual whose life was a train-wreck of his own making. Furthermore, through Matthew's life, Jesus wanted to show all of us that His kindness leads to repentance (Rom. 2:4) and His extension of grace, mercy, and love—when condemnation is the right, Provident judgment—changes people (Luke 18:9-14).

I have counseled numerous people with "Lightning Bolt Syndrome"; I have it, too. One afflicted with this spiritual hiccup expects to be zapped from Heaven when he or she falls short of God's expectations. As a result, in a vain effort to halt the electricity from the throne of God, I like to engage in Christian "magic" to atone for my mistakes.

I might strive harder in pastoral care; I might even vow to have more self-control in traffic when Mrs. McGillicuty drives thirty miles per hour in her 1970 Pacer and won't let me pass. While all of these changes are good character-building exercises, the motive behind them is fear of the lightning bolt. Such an approach to the Christian faith exhausts the individual and lacks joy. Consequently, the yoke remains.

Matthew's recovery, however, began the moment Jesus called him out of his tax racket and accepted him. Such Providential charity changed Matthew. Then, God used him tremendously. He preached the Gospel to those Jews in Judea after the ascension of his King and Messiah,[150] a testimony to the fact that he had come full circle in his life after exploiting them. You only need to open the New Testament and read the first book of it to see that Jesus majors in making the last first.

If that was true for Matthew, it is also true for you. God loves you. Let His kindness change you instead of creating God in your image when you mess up. Jesus took that wrath on the cross so you wouldn't have to. That's Divine love. Live in it.

PHILIP, THOMAS, AND JUDAS NOT ISCARIOT

How many times has someone asked you to pray for them, and you responded in the affirmative without doing it? Be honest. I know I have. Truth be known, we are often more interested in why someone is asking for our prayers than actually taking those concerns to the Heavenly Throne Room.

We do this because we subconsciously doubt the power of God. If we didn't, we would interrupt the person sharing the request and start interceding for them immediately. If we believed in God to intervene powerfully in a situation, we would claim the vision John had of the golden bowls containing "the prayers of the saints" (Rev. 5:8) as our own.

Doubting God's words, commands, and character came with severe consequences in the Old Covenant. Adam and Eve both did, and you know how their story ended. Moses couldn't even go into the Promised Land he was leading the Israelites to specifically because he doubted and disobeyed the Lord (Num. 20:8-11).

Jesus responded to great doubts with a more significant revelation of His character. Philip doubted, and Jesus fed five thousand people. God declared no moratorium on the future eternal inheritance of Thomas or Judas Not Iscariot for having the courage to say, "I'm not quite sure about all of this yet, Lord. Just give me a moment, please."

When they did, they were lovingly educated by the Divine Optometrist Himself—Jesus Christ our Lord—so they could see clearly. And behold, they certainly did! Philip took the Gospel to Greece, Syria, and Turkey.[151] Thomas' missionary endeavors to India paved the way for future missionaries like William Carey and Amy Carmichael there.[152] And Judas Not Iscariot confidently and boldly took the Gospel to Beirut, where he died a martyr for his blessed assurance.[153]

SIMON THE ZEALOT

A long time ago, Moses was on the summit of Mount Sinai and received these words from the Lord: "You shall not misuse the name of the Lord your God, for the Lord will not hold anyone guiltless who misuses his name" (Exod. 20:7).

Simon learned this command, the fourth of ten, was not limited to swearing. It also applied to folks like him who use the name of the Lord to get what they want: persecuting enemies to thwart similar persecution, for example.

The best way to spot someone who legitimately has a message to tell is to evaluate it in light of the Fruit of the Spirit (Gal. 6:22). You should listen to messengers from God who display them. Those who say one thing in God's name and act differently? Well, not so much.

The Zealot learned these lessons the hard way. While openly religious, he was also dangerously wrathful. Simon praised God out of one side of his mouth. Venomous curses, however, spewed out of the other when the "pagans" didn't see the world the way he did.

Like the crusaders in the Middle Ages, Simon used his mouth, sword, and political pontifications to carry the agenda he had for God to do in the world. He lacked not only a theological perspective, but also faith in God to control the outcome of a cultural clash.

Because He is slow to anger and quick to show His mercy triumphs over judgment, Jesus sought out Simon the Zealot and saved him. Then He commissioned Simon to start boasting about the only One who matters in the long run: Christ.

According to some Early Church traditions, he joined Judas Not Iscariot in Beirut, proclaiming the Gospel he learned from a merciful Savior.[154] Amazing, isn't it? This recovering terrorist was transformed into a missionary and died preaching the Gospel to those he would have murdered before Jesus conquered him. Such a metamorphosis in the Zealot's life came only through the power of Christ.

JUDAS ISCARIOT

Now we are left with the Son of Perdition. He doesn't seem to fit the copacetic, little narrative we've got going on. Think again. He fits quite well.

Do you remember that story in the first pages of the Bible about a serpent, a garden, and two people named Adam and Eve? You know the one where God wants fellowship with the two He created in His image? But the serpent, through deceit, seemingly succeeds in spoiling the plot by arousing suspicion regarding what God had said?

That same garden battle played out in the life of Christ and led to the cross. Using Judas Iscariot, Satan bruised the heel of Christ, causing Him to suffer immensely. God Himself said as much would happen in the first Messianic prophecy of the Bible (Gen. 3:15). Also, through the cross, Jesus won victory over any future "Judas endeavors" to foolishly try to thwart God from restoring humanity to Himself.

The same battle still rages in the hearts of people today. We all must decide which voice of the garden we are going to trust to construct the way we see the world and our purpose in it. Will we listen to the Iscariot serpent or Jesus? Thankfully, the disciples heard the voice of God, the One who called them from the parade route to the main attraction. They believed He could be trusted; I hope you will, too. Because they did, God used them to change the world. He will guide you to do the same.

WHY GOD USED THEM

When I was a lad, I won fifteen basketball championships in a row on my driveway court playing against an imaginary opponent: Michael Jordan Johnson, Jr. I beat him like a tied-up goat just to let him know I was supreme over him in my ability, power, status, and authority. My championships, however, stopped once I started playing against real people.

Why did God use those less-than-perfect men to change the world? To show the world what a supreme Savior, Who is equally benevolent and gracious, looks like through the work of redeemed rebels who display agape love to others. That's why. For two thousand years, Jesus has demonstrated His supremacy and goodness one heart at a time through the power of His pardon.

In his book *Mere Churchianity: Finding Your Way Back to Jesus-Shaped Spirituality*, Michael Spencer observes, "The human experience of weakness is God's blueprint for calling attention to the supremacy of his Son. When miserably failing people continue to belong to, believe in, and worship Jesus, God is happy."[155]

Look no further than the League of Pardoned Rebels that Jesus called His disciples for examples of miserably failing people. But make sure to look at them even longer to see God's blueprint for showing people Jesus in the way He changed them. He's still in that delightful business.

Jesus taught each of them how to love Him and love others. And He bet the farm that if they could, they would change the world. They did. Discipleship was God's answer to the problems in their world then. It's His answer to the issues we face as breathing human beings now, one Divinely solved in your life by moving from the parade route to the main attraction. For discipleship is nothing more than learning God's character and demonstrating it to others in love.

The door to the discipleship tent is wide open. Jesus has already paid your entry fee. Will you trust Him with your life and do what He says? Changing the world starts with you walking with Him a little more closely each day.

SOME QUESTIONS TO PONDER BEFORE MOVING ON

1. Read Mark 3:13-19. Which disciple do you identify with the most? Why?

2. Read Acts 9:10-19. How might God reveal His character and what He wants from us through relationships?

3. Read 1 Timothy 6:11-16. What were the areas of Timothy's life that required persevering challenges from Paul? In what ways have you been challenged to follow Jesus more closely through your reading?

Challenge

SO, THEREFORE, BASIN AND TOWEL DISCIPLESHIP

I GOT THE APPLICATION FOR the highly selective Cool Breeze Club during Mrs. Smart's class in the sixth grade. It said something to this effect: "You've been chosen to be a member of the Cool Breeze Club. To be a member, you must: (1) be a Cool Breeze; (2) wear a black Members Only Jacket; (3) tight roll your blue jeans; (4) wear Top Gun Shades at recess; (5) remain a Cool Breeze for life. Please sign."

Unfortunately, my kids kicked me out of the club the moment I chaperoned their school events and started waving at them while they were around their friends. That wasn't cool. It sure was funny, though.

Jesus was equally highly selective in whom He chose to institute His covenant. Our Lord was a Rabbi, Who called twelve *mathetes* to study, imitate, and obey Him. They left their families for an extended period to learn how to shine brightly as His people in the world. And doing that—as they would all learn—required submission in all facets of their lives.

Jesus' plan for His inner circle was much different than their reasoning for following Him. They saw privilege and a chance to be influential; He saw responsibility and an opportunity to be faithful. They were all selfishly competitive, ambitious, and insensitive. They were also prone to spiritual deafness and disloyalty, just like the disciple I look at in the mirror every day. To

Jesus, though, they were clay in His Divine hands, quite suitable for making spiritual pots useful to others. So are we.

If we're honest, we must admit that regardless of how long we've followed in Jesus' footsteps, that we still have much to learn about obedience. We must also confess that He still has much to mold in our lives. The more I reflect on the League of Pardoned Rebels Jesus called to follow Him, the more I'm convinced that we, as God's people, will collapse in a Humpty-Dumpty spill without a relational and caring dimension that goes hand-in-hand with our giftedness and skill. And the reason is simple: Jesus measures our character and spiritual maturity by how we relate to each other, not by what we accomplish. Because He's relational, Christ the Lord demands the same from us.

He demonstrated that by washing His disciple's feet the night before His death. Before Jesus suffered in anguish on the cross the next day, He thought they needed to learn about discipleship in its purest form, one seen most clearly with a bended knee by a water basin and a towel in hand. Do we see as clearly as Jesus did?

AN ACT OF THE WILL

Benjamin Disraeli, the great nineteenth century Prime Minister of the United Kingdom, once observed, "Nothing can withstand the power of the human will if it is willing to stake its very existence to the extent of its purpose."[156]

He would know; Disraeli staked his political career on improving the conditions of blue-collar workers throughout the UK.[157] Similarly, Jesus staked His hope for the world on the few He called to model one of His best methods for spiritual formation: foot washing. Why? It requires humility and meekness, not hubris and a desire to be first.

Serving others just like the greatest Teacher served the disciples is an act and exercise of the will. He won't put the towel in your hand and flick your ear until you dip it in the basin. You have to do it willingly, as an act of obedience to Him.

John tells us:

> The evening meal was in progress, and the devil had already prompted Judas, the son of Simon Iscariot, to betray Jesus. Jesus knew that the Father had put all things under his power, and that he had come from God and was returning to God; so he got up from the meal, took off his outer clothing, and wrapped a towel around his waist. After that, he poured water into a basin and began to wash his disciple's feet, drying them with the towel that was wrapped around him (John 13:2-5).

When read alongside the Passion Week accounts in the Synoptic Gospels, we learn that a dispute had broken out among the disciples about which of them would be the greatest in the Kingdom of Heaven. Jesus, however, didn't rise and rebuke them with His Divine words of heavenly wisdom. He did it with a lowly action; He washed their feet.

It was an impoverished action that revealed His meekness. And applying the towel in this manner while they were all beating their chests revealed they had forgotten the first line of the Sermon on the Mount: "Blessed are the poor in spirit, for theirs is the kingdom of heaven" (Matt. 5:2).

Admitting we are impoverished of spirit requires mighty courage and strength of character on our part in our me-first world. Such an admission, especially when followed by a demonstration, is love in action, not passive and in word only. Will we follow His example?

A CANAL FOR DIVINE MERCY

In Central America, the Panama Canal connects the Atlantic and Pacific Oceans. Without it, the goods you order online shipped from the coastlines of those two great bodies of water wouldn't arrive on your doorstep quickly or cheaply. Similarly, when we practice Basin-and-Towel Discipleship, we become a canal for the Divine mercies of God to flow to others.

Jesus commanded us to practice it: "You call me 'Teacher' and 'Lord,' and rightly so, for that is what I am. Now that I, your Lord and Teacher, have washed your feet, you also should wash one another's feet" (John 13:13-14).

If you don't like stinky feet, consider yourself in good company. I don't either. However, these words, voiced by our Lord in a musty room two thousand years ago, should force us to think long and hard about our tendency to want to win an argument in the name of Jesus instead of serving people. When we behave in such a way, we create Jesus in our image and then attach His name to our cause, not the other way around.

He cares about things like lepers, crosses, basins, towels, and feet. So should we. Because in the world of following Jesus, the last shall be first, and the first shall be at the back of the line. That's true now; it will be true tomorrow and always.

A DIVINE COMMAND

When I tell my son to brush his teeth, it's not a suggestion. It's a command I decree—quite often from my cushioned La-Z-Boy throne. I expect him to follow it. Similarly, Jesus not only commanded us to practice Basin-and-Towel Discipleship, He also beckons us to rank it on the same level as Baptism and Communion. He states, "I have set you an example that you should do as I have done for you" (John 13:15).

"That's not literal, preacher man. He means to serve people." I see that point, friend, and I agree with you to an extent. But here's the problem with that line of reasoning: He washed their feet because He wanted them to see what humility and serving the least looks like and because He tried to solve the inner conflict within each of them that collectively produced the rivalry and contention in the first place.

As a result, let's not punt this to the "Just Merely Spiritual Category" because the concept makes us uncomfortable. Instead, we need to interpret it exactly the way Jesus meant it: as an imperative command that denotes an obligation on our part to do as He instructed us.

How should we imitate the ethos of Jesus in our world right now? Let us start with the basin and the towel. Then people will know how valuable we really think they are in God's sight.

THE ROAD TO PROVIDENTIAL BLESSINGS

When we make Basin-and-Towel Discipleship our model for spiritual reproduction and do it, we also dispense and receive Providential blessings. Jesus concluded, "Very truly I tell you, no servant is greater than his master, nor is a messenger greater than the one who sent him. Now that you know these things, you will be blessed if you do them" (John 13:16-17).

I'm sure you've said amen a time or two after your preacher made a point that stirred your soul. The phrase "very truly" is emphatic, meaning "truly truly" or "amen amen." It also comes before the axiom. That means it matters not what we think because Jesus has already said amen. We either choose to obey or disobey.

Think about it like this: not once was Jesus insensitive to the needs of people who needed a spiritual doctor. Not once was He spiritually deaf or disloyal. Not once was He critical of people who placed their faith in Him because they knew they needed a Good Shepherd.

These adverse actions can cloud our thinking and render us ineffective for His purposes if we are not careful. They will also lock our knees from bending and paralyze our hands from serving. When they do, the basin remains empty, and the towel stays in the linen closet. But our Lord commanded us to start scrubbing.

Michael Card sang about it this way:

In an upstairs room, a parable,
Is just about to come alive.
And while they bicker about who's best,
With a painful glance, He'll silently rise.

Their Savior Servant must show them how,
Through the will of the water,
And the tenderness of the towel.
In any ordinary place, on any ordinary day.

This parable will live again.
When one will kneel and one will yield.
Our Savior Servant must show us how.
Through the will of the water and the tenderness of the towel.

And the call is to community,
The impoverished power that sets the soul free.
In humility, to take the vow,
That day after day we must take up the basin and the towel.[158]

Discipleship is merely imitating the way Jesus loved God and people—both of which are the essence of biblical testimony, from Genesis to Revelation. And my prayer is that the testimony will live again in your life more than it does now. The world depends on it. Jesus proved that to the rebels He pardoned and called disciples. Will we follow His example? Will we take up the towel and dip it in the basin?

SOME QUESTIONS TO PONDER BEFORE PUTTING YOUR BOOK ON THE SHELF

1. Read John 13:1-11. Why was Peter uncomfortable with Jesus washing his feet? Would having your feet washed or washing someone else's feet make you uncomfortable? Why or why not?

2. Read John 13:12-17. How does the practice demonstrate Christian leadership?

3. Pray and ask the Lord to show you how you can take up the basin and towel in your life by serving others.

FOR FURTHER READING

Connelly, Douglas. *The Twelve Disciples.* Life Guide Bible Studies. Downers Grove, IL: InterVarsity Press, 2014.

MacArthur, John. *Twelve Ordinary Men: How the Master Shaped His Disciples for Greatness, and What He Wants to Do with You.* Nashville, TN.: Thomas Nelson, 2002.

McBirnie, William Steuart. *The Search for the Twelve Apostles.* Carol Stream, IL: Tyndale, 2008.

Ruffin, C. Bernard. *The Twelve: The Lives of the Apostles After Calvary.* Huntington, IN: Our Sunday Visitor Publishing Division, 1984.

BIBLIOGRAPHY

PRIMARY SOURCES

de Voragine, Jacobus. *The Golden Legend: Readings on the Saints.* 7 volumes. Translated by William Granger Ryan. Princeton, NJ: Princeton University Press, 1993.

Eusebius of Caesarea. *The Church History of Eusebius.* Volume 1. *The Nicene and Post-Nicene.*

Fathers. Edited by Philip Schaff and Henry Wace. Peabody, MA: Hendrickson, 2004.

Hippolytus of Rome. *On the Twelve Apostles.* Volume 5. *The Ante-Nicene Fathers.* Edited by Alexander Roberts and James Donaldson. Peabody, MA: Hendrickson, 2004.

Holladay, William. *A Concise Hebrew and Aramaic Lexicon of the Old Testament.* Grand Rapids, MI: Eerdmans, 1988.

Irenaeus of Lyons. *Irenaeus Against Heresies.* Volume 1. *The Ante-Nicene Fathers.* Edited by Alexander Roberts and James Donaldson. Peabody, MASS: Hendrickson, 2004.

Jerome. *St. Jerome on Illustrious Men.* Translated by Thomas P. Halton. Washington, DC: Catholic University of America Press, 1999.

Newman, Barclay M., Jr. *A Concise Greek-English Dictionary of the New Testament.* Stuttgart, Germany: Deutsche Bibelgesellschaft, 1998.

Papias. *Fragments* in *The Ante-Nicene Fathers.* Volume 1. Edited by Alexander Roberts and James Donaldson. Peabody, MA: Hendrickson, 2004.

Roberts, Alexander and James Donaldson, eds. *The Acts of Philip.* Volume 8. *The Ante-Nicene Fathers.* Peabody, MA: Hendrickson Publishers, 2004.

Rogers, Cleon Jr. and Cleon Rogers, III. *The New Linguistic and Exegetical Key to the Greek New Testament.* Grand Rapids, MI: Zondervan, 1998.

The Works of Josephus: Complete and Unabridged. Translated by William Whiston. Peabody, MA: Hendrickson Publishers, 1987.

SECONDARY RESOURCES

Ackerman, Kenneth D. *Boss Tweed: The Rise and Fall of the Corrupt Pol Who Conceived the Soul of Modern New York.* Falls Church, VA: Carroll & Graff, 2005.

Anderson, Paul. "Can Any Good Thing Come From Nazareth? The Hometown of Jesus." *The Huffington Post Online,* March 22, 2017. https://www.huffingtonpost.com/entry/can-any-good-thing-come-from-nazareth-the-hometown_us_58d1f758e4b062043ad4ae1a (accessed September 4, 2018).

Andrew, S.J. "Melchizedek" in *The Dictionary of the Old Testament Pentateuch.* Edited by T. Desmond Alexander and David W. Baker. Downers Grove, IL: InterVarsity Press, 2003. 562-564.

Blake, Robert. *Disraeli.* London, England: Prion Books Limited, 1967.

Blomberg, Craig. "Jesus, Sinners, and Table Fellowship." *The Bulletin for Biblical Research* 19.1 (2009): 35-62.

Borchert, G.L. "Gnosticism" in *The Evangelical Dictionary of Theology*. Edited by Walter Elwell. Grand Rapids: MI: Baker Academic, 2001. 485-488.

Bosworth, F.F. *Christ the Healer.* Old Tappan, NJ: Fleming H. Revell, 1973.

Brooks, Philips. *Sermons.* New York, NY: E.P. Dutton & Company, 1838.

Brown, L.W. *The Indian Christians of St. Thomas.* Cambridge, UK: Cambridge University Press, 1982.

Bruce, F.F. *The Epistles to the Colossians, To Philemon, and to the Ephesians.* New International Commentary on the New Testament. Grand Rapids, MI: Eerdmans, 1984.

Carnegie, Dale. *How to Win Friends and Influence People.* New York, NY: Simon & Schuster, 1981. https://archive.org/details/DaleCarnegieHowToWinFriendsAndInfluencePeople_201803/page/nl3 (accessed December 11, 2018).

Chesterton, G.K. *Orthodoxy.* New York, NY: John Lane Company, 1908.

Chilton, B.D. "Judaism and the New Testament" in *The IVP Dictionary of the New Testament.*

Edited by Daniel G. Reid. Downers Grove, IL: InterVarsity Press, 2004. 603-616.

Connelly, Douglas. *The Twelve Disciples.* Life Guide Bible Studies. Downers Grove, IL: InterVarsity Press, 2014.

Cronwall, Judson and Stelman Smith. *The Exhaustive Dictionary of Bible Names.* Alachua, FL: Bridge-Logos, 1998.

Davies, Philip. *Scribes and Schools: The Canonization of the Hebrew Bible.* Louisville, KY: Westminster John Knox Press, 1998.

De Oliveria, Plinio Correa. "St. Thomas the Apostle." *Tradition in Action.* https://www.traditioninaction.org/SOD/j208sd_ThomasApostle_12-21.html (accessed December 18, 2018).

De Silva, D.A. "3 and 4 Maccabees" in *The Dictionary of New Testament Background.* Edited by Craig Evans and Stanley Porter. Downers Grove, IL: InterVarsity Press, 2000. 661-666.

Dolansky, Shawna. "The Truth(s) About Hanukkah." *The Huffington Post Online,* December 23, 2011. https://www.huffingtonpost.com/shawna-dolansky/the-truth-about-hanukah_b_1165708.html (accessed December 26, 2018).

Donahue, J.R. "Tax Collectors and Sinner." *Christian Biblical Quarterly* 33 (1971): 39-61.

Donne, John. "Death Be Not Proud" in *John Donne: The Major Works.* Edited by John Carey. Oxford, ENG: Oxford University Press, 2008.

Douglas, J.D. "Zebedee." *The New Bible Dictionary, s.v.* London, England: The InterVarsity Fellowship, 1963.

Doyle, Sir Arthur Conan. *The Adventures of Sherlock Holmes: Dover Thrift Editions.* Mineola, NY: Dover Publications, Inc., 2009.

Filson, Floyd. *The Gospel According to St. Matthew.* London, England: Adam and Charles Black, 1971.

Foster, Robert L. "Discipleship in the New Testament." *Society of Bible Literature's E-Newsletter for Public School Teachers,* 2011. https://www.sbl-site.org/assets/pdfs/tbv2i7_fosterdiscipleship.pdf (accessed May 23, 2018).

Garcia-Rivera, Alex. *A Wounded Innocence: Sketches for a Theology of Art.* Collegeville, MN: Liturgical Press, 2003.

Garret, D. A. "Levi, Levites" in *The Dictionary of the Old Testament Pentateuch.* Edited by T. Desmond Alexander and David W. Baker. Downers Grove, IL: InterVarsity Press, 2003. 519-522.

Giglio, Louie. "Louie Giglio #gls 14." *2014 Global Summit Leadership Session 8.* Online sermon, August 14, 2014. http://www.liveintentionally.org/2014/08/15/2014-global-leadership-summit-session-8-louie-giglio-gls14 (accessed August 12, 2019).

Gillingham, John. *Richard 1.* London, England: Yale University Press, 1999.

Gonzalez, Justo L. *The Story of Christianity: The Early Church to the Dawn of the Reformation.* New York, NY: HarperCollins, 2014.

Goodman, Martin. *Rome and Jerusalem: The Clash of Ancient Civilizations.* New York, NY: Vintage Books, 2008.

Grabbe, L.L. "1 and 2 Maccabees" in *The Dictionary of New Testament Background.* Edited by Craig Evans and Stanley Porter. Downers Grove, IL: InterVarsity Press, 2000. 657-661.

Graham, Billy. "Making a Difference in an Age of Crisis." *Decision Magazine,* July-August 2014. https://billygraham.org/decision-magazine/july-august-2014/making-a-difference-in-an-age-of-crisis (accessed November 12, 2018).

Grudem, Wayne. *Systematic Theology.* Grand Rapids, MI: Zondervan, 1994.

Guelich, R.A. "Mark, Gospel of" In *The IVP Dictionary of the New Testament.* Edited by Daniel G. Reid. Downers Grove, IL: InterVarsity Press, 2004. 770-784.

Hamilton, Victor P. *The Book of Genesis Chapters 18-50.* The New International Commentary on the Old Testament. Grand Rapids, MI: Eerdmans, 1995.

Harris, R. Laird, Gleason Archer, Jr., and Bruce Waltke. *Theological Wordbook of the Old Testament*. Chicago, IL: Moody Bible Institute, 1980.

Harrison, Ken. "There's a Surprising Connection Between Humility and Courage." Foxnews.com. https://www.foxnews.com/opinion/harrison-humility-courage (accessed August 16, 2019).

Hassel, R. Chris, Jr. *Shakespeare's Religious Language: A Dictionary*. New York, NY: Bloomsbury Publishing, 2015.

Heard, W.J and C.A. Evans. "Jewish Revolutionary Movements" in *The Dictionary of New Testament Background*. Edited by Craig Evans and Stanley Porter. Downers Grove, IL: InterVarsity Press, 2000. 936-947.

Jeffrey, Grant R. *The Signature of God*. Colorado Springs, CO: WaterBrook Press, 2010.

Kelly, William. "Napoleon's Testimony to Christ at St. Helena." *The Bible Treasury* 17 (1889).

Kipling, Rudyard. *Just So Stories*. Garden City, NY: The Country Life Press, 1912.

Kruse, Colin. *John*. The Tyndale New Testament Commentaries. Volume 4. Downers Grove, IL: InterVarsity Press, 2003.

Lazarski, Christopher. *Power Tends to Corrupt: Lord Action's Study of Liberty*. DeKalb, IL: Northern Illinois University Press, 2012.

Le Berre, Francois. *The Chameleon Handbook*. Hauppauge, NY: Barron's Educational Series, Inc., 2009.

Lewis, C.S. *The Chronicles of Narnia*. San Francisco, CA: HarperCollins Publishers, 1998.

Lewis, C.S. *The Great Divorce*. New York, NY: Touchstone, 1996.

Lukasiewicz, Jan. "On the Principle of Contradiction in Aristotle." *Review of Metaphysics* 24 (Jan. 1971): 485-509.

MacArthur, John. *Twelve Ordinary Men: How the Master Shaped His Disciples for Greatness and What He Wants to Do with You.* Nashville, TN: Thomas Nelson Publishers, 2002.

Manning, Brennan. *Abba's Child: The Cry of the Heart for Intimate Belonging.* Colorado Springs, CO: NavPress, 2015.

Martin, Ernest. *Restoring the Original Bible.* Portland, OR: The Associates for Scriptural Knowledge, 1994.

Marshall, I. Howard. *The Epistles of John.* The New International Commentary on the New Testament. Grand Rapids, MI: Eerdmans, 1978.

Mason, Mike. *Jesus: His Story in Stone.* Victoria, BC: Friesen Press, 2017.

McBirnie, William Steuart. *The Search for the Twelve Apostles.* Carol Stream, IL: Tyndale, 2008.

McClister, David. "The Scourging of Jesus." *Truth Magazine.* Volume 44. (January 2000): 11-12.

McDonald, David. *Heart of God: The Joy of Generous Living.* Jackson, MI: Westwinds Community Church Publications, 2009.

McKnight, Scot. "Matthew, Gospel of" in *The IVP Dictionary of the New Testament.* Edited by Daniel G. Reid. Downers Grove, IL: InterVarsity Press, 2004. 784-800.

Metzger, Bruce. *A Textual Commentary on the Greek New Testament.* Peabody, MA: Hendrickson Publishers, 2005.

Morgan, Robert J. *The Red Sea Rules: Ten God-Given Strategies for Difficult Times.* Nashville, TN: Thomas Nelson Publishers, 2014.

Morris, Leon. "Disciples of Jesus," in *Jesus of Nazareth: Essays on the Historical Jesus and New.*

Testament Chronology. Edited by Joel B. Green and Max Turner. Grand Rapids, MI: Eerdmans, 1994.

Morris, Leon. *The Gospel According to John. The New International Commentary on the New Testament.* Grand Rapids, MI: Eerdmans, 1995.

Nachman, Gerald. *Raised on Radio.* Berkley, CA: University of California Press, 1998.

Nickle, Keith F. *The Synoptic Gospels: An Introduction.* Louisville, KY: Westminster John Knox Press, 2001.

Platt, David. *Radical: Taking Back Your Faith from the American Dream.* Colorado Springs, CO: Multnomah, 2010.

Piper, John. "The Wisdom of Men and the Power of God." Desiringgod.org. Online Sermon, July 13, 1980. https://www.desiringgod.org/messages/the-wisdom-of-men-and-the-power-of-god (accessed November 14, 2018).

Poythress, Vern S. *Theophany: A Biblical Theology of God's Appearing.* Wheaton, IL: Crossway, 2018.

Riches, John, William R. Telford, and Christopher M. Tuckett. *The Synoptic Gospels.* Sheffield, England: Sheffield Academic Press, 2001.

Ritchie, Anne Isabella Thackerary. *Mrs. Dymond.* London, England: Smith, Elder & Company, 1885.

Rock, John T. "Boanerges, Sons of Thunder (Mark 3:17). *Journal of Biblical Literature* 100 (1981): 94-95.

Ruffin, Bernard C. *The Twelve: The Lives of the Apostles After Calvary.* Huntington, IN: Our Sunday Visitor Publishing, 1984.

"Saint Jude Thaddeus." Catholicsaints.info. https://catholicsaints.info/saint-jude-thaddeus (accessed October 2, 2019).

Santayana, George. *The Life of Reason: The Phases of Human Progress.* New York, NY: Dover Publications, Inc., 2005. http://www.gutenberg.org/files/15000/15000-h/15000-h.htm (accessed October 2, 2019).

Sarkis, Stephanie A. "Twenty Five Quotes on Willpower." Psychologytoday.com, February 8, 2011. https://www.psychologytoday.com/us/blog/here-there-and-everywhere/201102/25-quotes-willpower (accessed October 2, 2019).

Schaff, Philip. *History of the Apostolic Church: With a General Introduction to Church History.* New York, NY: Charles Scribner, 1853.

Shakespeare, William. *The Third Part of King Henry the Sixth.* Act 5. Scene 7. http://shakespeare.mit.edu/3henryvi/3henryvi.5.7.html (accessed September 17, 2019).

Shakespeare, William. *The Tragedy of Hamlet, Prince of Denmark.* New York, NY: Grosset & Dunlap, 1909.

Shellnut, Kate. "Paige Patterson Fired By Southwestern, Stripped of Retirement Benefits." Christianitytoday.com, May 30, 2018. https://www.christianitytoday.com/news/2018/may/paige-patterson-fired-southwestern-baptist-seminary-sbc.html (accessed June 6, 2018).

Shurkin, Joel N. "How Many People Heard the Sermon on the Mount? Or the Gettysburg Address?" Foxnews.com, December 10, 2013. http://www.foxnews.com/science/2013/12/10/how-many-people-heard-sermon-on-mount.html (accessed August 15, 2019).

Smith, Douglas. *Rasputin: Faith, Power, and the Twilight of the Romanovs.* New York, NY: Farrar, Straus and Giroux, 2016.

Smith, William. *Smith's Bible Dictionary*, s.v. "Alphaeus." https://www.biblestudytools.com/dictionaries/smiths-bible-dictionary/alphaeus.html (accessed October 2, 2019).

Spencer, Michael. *Mere Churchianity: Finding Your Way Back to Jesus-Shaped Spirituality*. Colorado Springs, CO: WaterBrook Press, 2010.

Spurgeon, Charles Haddon. *Spurgeon's Sermons*. Volume 2. Grand Rapids, MI: Baker Book House, 1983.

Strong, James. *The Strongest Strongs Exhaustive Concordance of the Bible*. Grand Rapids, MI: Zondervan, 2001.

Thompson, Francis. *The Hound of Heaven and Other Poems*. Wellesley, MASS: Branden Books, 2017.

Tongue, D.H. "Light" in *The Evangelical Dictionary of Theology*. Edited by Walter A. Elwell. Grand Rapids, MI: Baker Academic, 2007. 692-693.

Tozer, A.W. *Knowledge of the Holy: Drawing Close to God By Knowing His Attributes*. Zeeland, MI: Reformed Church Publications, 2015.

Vadakkekara, Benedict. *Origin of India's St. Thomas Christians: A Historiographical Critique*. Delhi: Media House, 1995.

Vogt, Katja. "Ancient Skepticism." *The Stanford Encyclopedia of Philosophy*. June 20, 2018. https://plato.stanford.edu/entries/skepticism-ancient (accessed December 12, 2018).

Volkmer, W.K. *These Things: A Reference Manual for Discipleship*. San Antonio, TX: The Passionate Few, 2017.

Wachsmann, Shelley. *The Sea of Galilee Boat: An Extraordinary 2000 Year Old Discovery*. New York, NY: Plenum, 1995.

Wachtel, Roger. *The Tomb of the Unknown Soldier: Cornerstones of Freedom.* New York, NY: Children's Press, 2009.

Wagner, C. Peter. *Acts of the Holy Spirit.* Ventura, CA: Regal Books, 2000.

Jackson, Kathy, ed. *Walt Disney: Conversations.* Jackson, MS: University of Mississippi Press, 2006.

Whitacre, R.A. "Vine, Fruit of the Vine" in *Dictionary of Jesus and the Gospels.* Edited by Joel B. Green. Downers Grove, IL: InterVarsity Press, 2013. 866-867.

Wiersbe, Warren. *Listening to the Giants.* Grand Rapids, MI: Baker Book House, 1980.

Wilde, Oscar. *Lady Windermere's Fan: A Play About A Good Woman.* London, England: Elkin Mathews and John Lane, 1893.

Wilkins, Michael J. *Matthew. The NIV Application Commentary.* Grand Rapids, MI: Zondervan, 2004.

Willard, Dallas. *The Spirit of the Disciplines: Understanding How God Changes Lives.* San Francisco: Harper Collins, 1990.

Williams, Garry. "10 Things You Should Know About the Love of God." *Crossway.org,* July 11, 2016. https://www.crossway.org/articles/10-things-you-should-know-about-the-love-of-god (accessed August 20, 2019).

Williamson, P.R. "Abraham." *The Dictionary of the Old Testament Pentateuch.* Edited by T. Desmond Alexander and David W. Baker. Downers Grove, IL: InterVarsity Press, 2003. 11-18.

Wirt, William. *Sketches of the Life and Character of Patrick Henry.* Freeport, NY: Books for Libraries Press, 1970.

Wylie, John Thomas. *A Brief New Testament Survey on the Life of Jesus Christ.* Bloomington, IN: AuthorHouse, 2016.

Zieve, Tamara. "Archaeologists Uncover Gate to Biblical City of Zer." Jerusalem Post Online, July 8, 2018. https://www.jpost.com/Israel-News/Archaeologists-uncover-gate-to-biblical-city-of-Zer-561941 (accessed July 11, 2018).

DISCOGRAPHY

MOVIES

Amazing Grace. Directed by Michael Apted. Burbank: FourBoys Films, Walden Media, Bristol.

Bay Productions, Ingenious Film Partners and Road Side Attraction Productions, 2006. DVD.

E.T. the Extra-Terrestrial. Directed by Steven Spielberg. Universal City: Universal Pictures, 1982. DVD.

Good Will Hunting. Directed by Gus Van Sant. Los Angeles: Be Gentleman Productions, 1997. DVD.

Rocky. Directed by John G. Avildsen. Los Angeles: Chartoff-Winkler Productions, 1976. DVD.

Star Wars. Directed by George Lucas. San Francisco: Lucasfilm Ltd., 1977. DVD.

The Wizard of Ox. Directed by Victor Fleming. Beverly Hills: Metro-Goldwyn-Mayer, 1939. DVD. Warner Home Video, 2013.

MUSIC

Borger, Joyce. "Father Abraham Had Many Sons." *Sing With Me.* Grand Rapids, MI: Christian Schools International, 2006.

Card, Michael. "The Basin and Towel." *Poiema*. The Sparrow Corporation. 2. 1994. Compact disc.

Cash, Johnny. "A Boy Named Sue." *Quentin: Legacy Edition*. Columbia Records. 5. 1969. Compact disc.

Crickets, The. "I Fought the Law." *In Style with the Crickets*. Coral Records. 11. 1960. Compact disc.

Mullins, Rich. "The Love of God." *Never Picture Perfect*. Reunion Records. 3. Side 2. 1989. Cassette tape.

Sims, Walter Hines, ed. *The Baptist Hymnal*. Nashville, TN: Lifeway, 2008.

    Anonymous. "I Have Decided to Follow Jesus." 434.

    Bradbury, William B. "Just As I Am, Without One Plea." 435.

    Crosby, Fanny J. "To God Be the Glory Great Things He Has Done." 28.

    Duffield, George Jr. "Stand Up for Jesus." 657.

    Fawcett, John. "Blessed be the Tie." 389.

    Gabriel, Charles H. "I Stand Amazed in the Presence." 237.

    Luther, Martin. "A Mighty Fortress Is Our God." 656.

    Newton, John. "Amazing Grace! How Sweet the Sound." 104.

    Warner, Anna B. "Jesus Loves Me." 651.

    Watts, Isaac. "Joy to the World! The Lord Is Come." 181.

    Woolston, C.H. "Jesus Loves the Little Children." 651.

    Yates, John H. "Faith is the Victory." 520.

Smith, Michael W. "Secret Ambition." *i 2 (Eye)*. Reunion Records. 2. 1988. Compact disc.

Toad the Wet Sprocket. "Fly from Heaven." *Dulcinea*. Columbia Records. 1. 1994. Compact disc.

TELEVISION

Killing Jesus. Directed by Christopher Menaul. Los Angeles, CA: National Geographic Distribution and Scott Free Productions, 2015. Television show.

Sesame Street #24.33. Produced by Dulcy Singer. Queens, NY: Kaufman Astoria Studios, 1992. Television show.

ENDNOTES

1. *The Wizard of Oz,* directed by Victor Fleming (Metro-Goldwyn-Mayer, 1939), DVD (2013).

2. Barclay M. Newman, Jr., *A Concise Greek-English Dictionary of the New Testament,* s.v. "maqhthj, ou," (Stuttgart, Germany: Deutsche Bibelgesellschaft, 1998), 110.

3. Fanny J. Crosby, "To God Be the Glory Great Things He Has Done," in *The Baptist Hymnal,* ed. Walter Hines Sims (Nashville, TN: Lifeway, 2008), 28.

4. David Platt, *Radical: Taking Back Your Faith from the American Dream* (Colorado Springs, CO: Multnomah, 2010), pp. 10-11.

5. Wayne Grudem, *Systematic Theology: An Introduction to Biblical Doctrine* (Grand Rapids, MI: Zondervan, 2000), 1241.

6. Joyce Borger, "Father Abraham Had Many Sons," in *Sing With Me* (Grand Rapids, MI: Christian Schools International, 2006), 68.

7. Anonymous, "I Have Decided to Follow Jesus," in *The Baptist Hymnal,* ed. Walter Hines Sims (Nashville, TN: Lifeway, 2008), 434.

8. Barclay M. Newman Jr., *A Concise Greek-English Dictionary of the New Testament,* s.v. "petra, aj," (Stuttgart, Germany: Deutsche Bibelgesellschaft, 1998), 141-142.

9. Cleon L. Rogers Jr. and Cleon L. Rogers, III, *The New Linguistic and Exegetical Key to the Greek New Testament* (Grand Rapids, MI: Zondervan, 1998), 8.

10 William L. Holladay, *A Concise Hebrew and Aramaic Lexicon of the Old Testament*, s.v. "~hrba" and "~rba" (Grand Rapids, MI: Eerdmans, 1988), 3.

11 Ibid, s.v. "bq[y" and "larfy," 138, 145.

12 John H. Yates, "Faith is the Victory," in *The Baptist Hymnal*, ed. Walter Hines Sims (Nashville, TN: Lifeway, 2008), 520.

13 James Strong, *The Strongest Strongs Exhaustive Concordance of the Bible*, s.v. "1568. Ekqambew, ekthambeo," (Grand Rapids, MI: Zondervan, 2001), 1494.

14 John T. Rook, "Boanerges, Sons of Thunder (Mark 3:17)," *Journal of Biblical Literature* 100 (1981):94-95.

15 Ernest Martin, *Restoring the Original Bible*, (Portland, OR: The Associates for Scriptural Knowledge, 1994), 311.

16 J. D. Douglas (ed.), "Zebedee," *The New Bible Dictionary* (London: The Inter-Varsity Fellowship, 1963), 1354.

17 Shelley Wachsmann, *The Sea of Galilee Boat: An Extraordinary 2000 Year Old Discovery* (New York, NY: Plenum, 1995).

18 Ibid.

19 Mike Mason, *Jesus: His Story in Stone* (Victoria, BC: Friesen Press, 2017), 164.

20 *Antiquities of the Jews* 6.11.19, in *The Works of Josephus: Complete and Unabridged*, trans. William Whiston (Peabody, Mass.: Hendrickson Publishers, 1987), 169.

21 George Duffield Jr., "Stand Up for Jesus," in *The Baptist Hymnal*, Walter Hines Sims, Ed. (Nashville, TN: Lifeway, 2008), 657.

22 Kenneth D. Ackerman, *Boss Tweed: The Rise and Fall of the Corrupt Pol Who Conceived the Soul of Modern New York* (Falls Church, VA: Carroll & Graff, 2005), 1-6.

23 Kate Shellnut, "Paige Patterson Fired by Southwestern, Stripped of Retirement Benefits," *Christianity Today International*, https://www.christianitytoday.com/news/2018/may/paige-patterson-fired-southwestern-baptist-seminary-sbc.html (accessed June 6, 2018).

24 Christopher Lazarski, *Power Tends to Corrupt: Lord Action's Study of Liberty* (DeKalb, IL: Northern Illinois University Press, 2012), 2.

25 *Merriam Webster's Online Dictionary*, s.v. "Humility," https://www.merriam-webster.com/dictionary/humility (Accessed September 3, 2019).

26 Philips Brooks, *Sermons* (New York: NY: E.P. Dutton & Company, 1838), 340.

27 Louie Giglio, "Louie Giglio #gls 14," *2014 Global Summit Leadership Session 8* (accessed August 12, 2019).

28 Leon Morris, *The Gospel According to John, The New International Commentary on the New Testament* (Grand Rapids, MI: Eerdmans, 1995), 555.

29 Ibid.

30 John Riches, William R. Telford, and Christopher M. Tuckett, *The Synoptic Gospels* (Sheffield, England: Sheffield Academic Press, 2001), 9.

31 Michael W. Smith, "Secret Ambition," *i 2 (Eye)*, Reunion Record, 2, 1988, compact disc.

32 Ken Harrison, "There's a Surprising Connection Between Humility and Courage," Foxnews.com, April 20, 2019, https://www.foxnews.com/opinion/harrison-humility-courage (accessed August 16, 2019).

33 Joel N. Shurkin, "How Many People Heard the Sermon on the Mount? Or the Gettysburg Address?," Foxnews.com, http://www.foxnews.com/science/2013/12/10/how-many-people-heard-sermon-on-mount.html (accessed August 15, 2019).

34 C.H. Woolston, "Jesus Loves the Little Children," in *The Baptist Hymnal*, Walter Hines Sims, Ed. (Nashville, TN: Lifeway, 2008), 651.

35 I. Howard Marshall, *The Epistles of John, The New International Commentary on the New Testament* (Grand Rapids, MI: Eerdmans, 1978), 215.

36 Garry Williams, "10 Things You Should Know About the Love of God," Crossway.org, https://www.crossway.org/articles/10-things-you-should-know-about-the-love-of-god (accessed August 20, 2019).

37 Ibid.

38 *Against Heresies* 3.1—available in *Ante-Nicene Fathers,* vol 1, eds., Alexander Roberts and James Donaldson (Peabody, MA: Hendrickson Publishers, 2004), 414.

39 John Gillingham, *Richard I* (London, England: Yale University Press, 1999), 222-253.

40 Kathy Jackson, ed., *Walt Disney: Conversations* (Jackson, MS: University of Mississippi Press, 2006), 20-33.

41 The Crash Test Dummies, "Superman's Song," *The Ghosts That Haunt Me,* 3, BMG/Arista Records, 1991, compact disc.

42 The Crickets, "I Fought the Law," *In Style with the Crickets,* 11, Coral Records, 1960.

43 *The Life of Flavius Josephus* 71.398-406 in *The Works of Josephus: Complete and Unabridged* (24-25).

44 Tamara Zieve, "Archaeologists Uncover Gate to Biblical City of Zer," *Jerusalem Post Online,* July 8, 2018, https://www.jpost.com/Israel-News/Archaeologists-uncover-gate-to-biblical-city-of-Zer-561941 (accessed July 11, 2018).

45 Rich Mullins, "The Love of God," *Songs 2,* 13, Reunion Records, 1999, compact disc.

46 A.W. Tozer in In *These Things: A Reference Manual for Discipleship*, W.K. Volkmer (San Antonio, TX: The Passionate Few, 2017), 171.

47 David McDonald, *Heart of God: The Joy of Generous Living* (Jackson, MI: Westwinds Community Church Publications, 2009), 82.

48 Francis Thompson, *The Hound of Heaven and Other Poems* (Wellesley, Mass.: Branden Books, 2017), 6.

49 *Merriam Webster's Online Dictionary, s.v.* "Metamorphosis," https://www.merriam-webster.com/dictionary/metamorphosis (Accessed July 11, 2018).

50 William L. Holladay, *A Concise Hebrew and Aramaic Lexicon of the Old Testament, s.v.* "la" and "!jn" (Grand Rapids, MI: Eerdmans, 1988), 15, 249.

51 Paul Anderson, "Can Any Good Thing Come From Nazareth? The Hometown of Jesus," The Huffington Post Online, https://www.huffingtonpost.com/entry/can-any-good-thing-come-from-nazareth-the-hometown_us_58d1f758e4b062043ad4ae1a (accessed September 4, 2018).

52 C.S. Lewis, *The Magician's Nephew*, in *The Chronicles of Narnia* (San Francisco, CA: HarperCollins Publishers, 1998), 104.

53 Leon Morris, *The Gospel According to John, The New International Commentary on the New Testament* (Grand Rapids, MI: Eerdmans, 1995), 146.

54 William B. Bradbury, "Just As I Am, Without One Plea," in *The Baptist Hymnal*, Walter Hines Sims, Ed. (Nashville, TN: Lifeway, 2008), 435.

55 William L. Holladay, *A Concise Hebrew and Aramaic Lexicon of the Old Testament, s.v.* "!tm" and "hwhy" (Grand Rapids, MI: Eerdmans, 1988), 222, 130.

56 Fanny Crosby, "To God Be the Glory Great Things He Has Done," in *The Baptist Hymnal*, Walter Hines Sims, Ed. (Nashville, TN: Lifeway, 2008), 28.

57 Cleon L. Rogers Jr. and Cleon L. Rogers, III, *The New Linguistic and Exegetical Key to the Greek New Testament* (Grand Rapids, MI: Zondervan, 1998), 20.

58 Floyd Filson, *The Gospel According to St. Matthew* (London, England: Adam and Charles Black, 1971), 84.

59 J.R. Donahue, "Tax Collectors and Sinner," in *Christian Biblical Quarterly* 33 (1971): 39-61.

60 *Oxford Living Dictionaries, s.v.,* "Boast," https://en.oxforddictionaries.com/definition/boast (accessed November 12, 2018).

61 Billy Graham, "Making a Difference in an Age of Crisis," *Decision Magazine*, https://billygraham.org/decision-magazine/july-august-2014/making-a-difference-in-an-age-of-crisis (accessed November 12, 2018).

62 A.W. Tozer, *Knowledge of the Holy: Drawing Close to God by Knowing His Attributes* (Zeeland, MI: Reformed Church Publications, 2015), 84.

63 Michael J. Wilkins, *Matthew, The NIV Application Commentary* (Grand Rapids, MI: Zondervan, 2004).

64 John Piper, "The Wisdom of Men and the Power of God," Desiringgod.org, https://www.desiringgod.org/messages/the-wisdom-of-men-and-the-power-of-god (accessed November 14, 2018).

65 John Newton, "Amazing Grace! How Sweet the Sound," in *The Baptist Hymnal*, 104.

66 *Amazing Grace,* directed by Michael Apted (Burbank, CA: FourBoys Films, Walden Media, Bristol Bay Productions, Ingenious Film Partners and Road Side Attraction Productions, 2007), DVD.

67 *Sesame Street #24.33,* produced by Dulcy Singer (Queens, NY: Kaufman Astoria Studios, 1992), television show.

68 Barclay M. Newman, *A Concise Greek-English Dictionary of the New Testament,* s.v. "Didumoj, ou," (Stuttgart, Germany: Deutsche Bibelgesellschaft, 1988), 45.

69 F.F. Bosworth, *Christ the Healer* (Old Tappan, NJ: Fleming H. Revell, 1973), 12-13.

70 Alex Garcia-Rivera, *A Wounded Innocence: Sketches for a Theology of Art* (Collegeville, MN: Liturgical Press, 2003), 120-123.

71 Dale Carnegie, *How to Win Friends and Influence People* (New York: NY: Simon & Schuster, 1981), https://archive.org/details/DaleCarnegieHowToWinFriendsAndInfluencePeople_201803/page/n13 (accessed December 11, 2018).

72 Cleon L. Rogers Jr and Cleon L. Rogers, III, *The New Linguistic and Exegetical Key to the Greek New Testament* (Grand Rapids, MI: Zondervan, 1998), 172.

73 Martin Luther, "A Mighty Fortress Is Our God," in *The Baptist Hymnal,* Walter Hines Sims, Ed. (Nashville, TN: Lifeway, 2008), 656.

74 Katja Vogt's "Ancient Skepticism," in *The Stanford Encyclopedia of Philosophy,* https://plato.stanford.edu/entries/skepticism-ancient (accessed December 12, 2018).

75 Toad the Wet Sprocket, "Fly from Heaven," *Dulcinea,* 1, Columbia Records, 1994, compact disc.

76 John Fawcett, "Blessed be the Tie," in *The Baptist Hymnal,* 389.

77 Charles Haddon Spurgeon, *Spurgeon's Sermons,* Volume 2 (Grand Rapids, MI: Baker Book House, 1983), 90.

78 Victor P. Hamilton, *The Book of Genesis Chapters 18-50, The New International Commentary on the Old Testament* (Grand Rapids, MI: Eerdmans, 1995), 13.

79 David McClister, "The Scourging of Jesus," *Truth Magazine,* vol. 44 (January 2000): 11-12.

80 Newman, *s.v.* "kurij, ou," 105.

81 Colin Kruse, *John, The Tyndale New Testament Commentaries*, vol. 4 (Downers Grove, IL: InterVarsity Press, 2003), 379.

82 Leon Morris, *The Gospel According to John, The New International Commentary on the New Testament* (Grand Rapids, MI: Eerdmans, 1995), 754.

83 Henry Drummond, quoted in Warren W. Wiersbe, *Listening to the Giants*, (Grand Rapids, MI: Baker Book House, 1980), 115-116.

84 Eusebius of Caesarea, *Eusebius' Church History 3.1.1.*, Volume 1, *Nicene and Post-Nicene Fathers,* eds. Philip Schaff and Henry Wace (Peabody, MA: Hendrickson, 2004), 132.

85 L.W. Brown, *The Indian Christians of St. Thomas* (Cambridge, UK: Cambridge University Press, 1982), 49-59.

86 Plinio Correa de Oliveria's "St. Thomas the Apostle," Traditioninaction.org (accessed December 18, 2018).

87 Anna B. Warner, "Jesus Loves Me," in *The Baptist Hymnal*, 651.

88 James Strong, *The Strongest Strongs Exhaustive Concordance of the Bible*, s.v. "Zeal," (Grand Rapids, MI: Zondervan, 2001), 7031.

89 Ibid.

90 Shawna Dolansky, "The Truth(s) About Hanukkah," Huffington Post Online, https://www.huffingtonpost.com/shawna-dolansky/the-truth-about-hanukah_b_1165708.html (accessed December 26, 2018).

91 W.J. Heard and C.A. Evans, "Jewish Revolutionary Movements," in *Dictionary of New Testament Background* (Downers Grove, IL: InterVarsity Press, 2000), 945.

92 *Antiquities of the Jews 18.1.6.*, in *The Works of Josephus: Complete and Unabridged*, trans. William Whiston (Peabody, Mass.: Hendrickson Publishers, 1987), 477.

93 William Wirt, *Sketches of the Life and Character of Patrick Henry* (Freeport, NY: Books for Libraries Press, 1970), 110.

94 C.S. Lewis, *The Great Divorce* (New York, NY: Touchstone, 1996), 70-71.

95 Martin Goodman, *Rome and Jerusalem: The Clash of Ancient Civilizations* (New York, NY: Vintage Books, 2008), 407).

96 Wirt, 110.

97 William Kelly, "Napoleon's Testimony to Christ at St. Helena," in *The Bible Treasury* 17 (1889).

98 William Newell and Daniel Towner, "At Calvary," in *The Baptist Hymnal* (Nashville, TN: Lifeway, 2008), 245.

99 Jacobus de Voragine, *The Golden Legend: Readings on the Saints*, vol. 6, trans. William Granger Ryan (Princeton, NJ: Princeton University Press, 1993), 35-38.

100 Roger Wachtel, *The Tomb of the Unknown Soldier: Cornerstones of Freedom* (New York, NY: Children's Press, 2009), 1.

101 Barclay M. Newman, *A Concise Greek-English Dictionary of the New Testament*, s.v. "mikroj, a, on" (Stuttgart, Germany: Deutsche Bibelgesellschaft, 1988), 117.

102 Ibid.

103 John MacArthur, *Twelve Ordinary Men: How the Master Shaped His Disciples for Greatness and What He Wants to Do with You* (Nashville, TN: Thomas Nelson, 2002), 171-172.

104 Ibid, 172.

105 Gerald Nachman, *Raised on Radio* (Berkley, CA: University of California Press, 1998), 200.

106 G.K. Chesterton, *Orthodoxy* (New York, NY: John Lane Company, 1908), 29.

107 Newman, *s.v.* "musthrion, ou," 119.

108 F.F. Bruce, *The Epistles to the Colossians, to Philemon, and to the Ephesians,* NICNT (Grand Rapids, MI: Eerdmans, 1984), 310-321.

109 Oscar Wilde, *Lady Windermere's Fan: A Play About A Good Woman* (London, England: Elkin Mathews and John Lane, 1893), Act 1.

110 William Shakespeare, *The Tragedy of Hamlet, Prince of Denmark* (New York, NY: Grosset & Dunlap, 1909), Act 3, Part 4.

111 John Donne, "Death Be Not Proud," in *John Donne: The Major Works,* ed. John Carey (Oxford, England: Oxford University Press, 2008), 175.

112 Jan Lukasiewicz, "On the Principle of Contradiction in Aristotle," *Review of Metaphysics* 24 (Jan 1971): 485-509.

113 William Smith, "Alphaeus," *Smith's Bible Dictionary Online, s.v.* https://www.biblestudytools.com/dictionaries/smiths-bible-dictionary/alphaeus.html (accessed October 2, 2019).

114 Wachtel, 45.

115 Francois Le Berre, *The Chameleon Handbook* (Hauppauge, NY: Barron's Educational Series, Inc., 2009), 2.

116 Sir Arthur Conan Doyle, *The Adventures of Sherlock Holmes: Dover Thrift Editions* (Mineola, NY: Dover Publications, Inc., 2009).

117 William Shakespeare, "The Tragedy of Hamlet, Prince of Denmark" (1909): Part 3.

118 William L. Holladay, *A Concise Hebrew and Aramaic Lexicon of the Old Testament*, s.v. "hdy" (Grand Rapids, Eerdmans, 1988), 128.

119 Barclay M. Newman, *A Concise Greek-English Dictionary of the New Testament*, s.v. "Iskariwq" (Stuttgart, Germany, 1988), 87.

120 Holladay, *s.v.* "arq," 323.

121 William Shakespeare, "The Third Part of King Henry the Sixth," Act 5, Scene 7, http://shakespeare.mit.edu/3henryvi/3henryvi.5.7.html (accessed September 17, 2019).

122 B.D. Chilton, "Judaism and the New Testament," in *The IVP Dictionary of the New Testament* (Downers Grove, IL: InterVarsity Press, 2004), 610.

123 Douglas Smith, *Rasputin: Faith, Power, and the Twilight of the Romanovs* (New York, NY: Farrar, Straus and Giroux, 2016), 65-107.

124 Brennan Manning, *Abba's Child: The Cry of the Heart for Intimate Belonging* (Colorado Springs, CO: NavPress, 2015), xiv.

125 George Santayana, *The Life of Reason: The Phases of Human Progress*, http://www.gutenberg.org/files/15000/15000-h/15000-h.htm (accessed October 2, 2019).

126 *E.T. the Extra-Terrestrial*, directed by Steven Spielberg (Universal City: Universal Pictures, 1982), DVD (2012).

127 *Rocky*, directed by John G. Avildsen (Los Angeles: Chartoff-Winkler Productions, 1976), DVD (2016).

128 *Star Wars*, directed by George Lucas (San Francisco: Lucasfilm Ltd., 1977), DVD (2015).

129 John MacArthur, *Twelve Ordinary Men: How the Master Shaped His Disciples for Greatness and What He Wants to Do with You* (Nashville, TN: Thomas Nelson, 2002), 178.

130 Bruce Metzger, *A Textual Commentary on the Greek New Testament* (Peabody, MA: Hendrickson Publishers, 2005), 21.

131 "Saint Jude Thaddeus," *Catholicsaints.info*, https://catholicsaints.info/saint-jude-thaddeus (accessed October 2, 2019).

132 John Thomas Wylie, *A Brief New Testament Survey on the Life of Jesus Christ* (Bloomington, IN: AuthorHouse, 2016), 81.

133 Ibid.

134 Charles H. Gabriel, "I Stand Amazed in the Presence," in *The Baptist Hymnal*, Walter Hines Sims, Ed. (Nashville, TN: Lifeway, 2008), 237.

135 Isaac Watts, "Joy to the World! The Lord Is Come," in *The Baptist Hymnal*, 181.

136 Matthew 26:29; Mark 14:25; Luke 22:18; and John 15:1, 4-5.

137 Isaiah 3:14; 5:1-7; Jeremiah 12:10.

138 R.A. Whitacre, "Vine, Fruit of the Vine," *Dictionary of Jesus and the Gospels*, ed. Joel B. Green (Downers Grove, IL: InterVarsity Press, 2013), 867.

139 Rudyard Kipling, *Just So Stories* (Garden City, NY: The Country Life Press, 1912), 63.

140 Robert J. Morgan, *The Red Sea Rules: Ten God-Given Strategies for Difficult Times* (Nashville, TN: Thomas Nelson Publishers, 2014), 11-12.

141 Martin Luther, "A Mighty Fortress Is Our God," in *The Baptist Hymnal*, ed. Walter Hines Sims (Nashville, TN: Lifeway, 2008), 656.

142 Eusebius of Caesarea, *Eusebius' Church History 3.1.1.* (2004), 132.

143 Ibid.

144 Jacobus de Voragine, *The Golden Legend: Readings on the Saints,* vol. 1, trans. William Granger Ryan (Princeton, NJ: Princeton University Press, 1993), 13-20.

145 *Killing Jesus,* directed by Christopher Menaul (Los Angeles, CA: National Geographic Distribution and Scott Free Productions, 2015), television show.

146 Philip Schaff, *History of the Apostolic Church: With a General Introduction to Church History* (New York, NY: Charles Scribner, 1853), 389.

147 Hilarie and James Cornwell, *Saints, Signs, and Symbols* (New York: Morehouse Publishing, 2009), 49.

148 G.L Borchert, "Gnosticism," in *The Evangelical Dictionary of Theology,,* Walter Elwell, ed. (Grand Rapids, MI: Baker Academic, 2001), 487.

149 Eusebius of Caesarea, *Eusebius' Church History 5.10.3* (2004), 225.

150 Irenaeus of Lions, *Against Heresies 3.1.1.,* in *Ante-Nicene Fathers,* vol. 1, eds., Alexander Roberts and James Donaldson (Peabody, MA: Hendrickson Publishers, 2004), 414.

151 "The Acts of Philip," in *The Ante-Nicene Fathers,* vol. 8, eds., Alexander Roberts and James Donaldson (Peabody, MA: Hendrickson Publishers, 2004), 497.

152 Benedict Vadakkekara, *Origin of India's St. Thomas Christians: A Historiographical Critique* (Delhi: Media House, 1995).

153 De Voragine, *The Golden Legend: Readings on the Saints,* vol. 6, 35-38.

154 Ibid.

155 Michael Spencer, *Mere Churchianity: Finding Your Way Back to Jesus-Shaped Spirituality* (Colorado Springs, CO: WaterBrook Press, 2010), 145.

156 Stephanie A. Sarkis, "Twenty Five Quotes on Willpower," Psychologytoday.com, https://www.psychologytoday.com/us/blog/here-there-and-everywhere/201102/25-quotes-willpower (accessed October 2, 2019).

157 Robert Blake, *Disraeli* (London, England: Prion Books Limited, 1967), 272-273.

158 Michael Card, "The Basin and Towel," *Poiema*, 2, The Sparrow Corporation, 1994, compact disc.

For more information about
Derrick West
and
The League of Pardoned Rebels
please connect at:

www.dderrickwest.wordpress.com
www.facebook.com/theleagueofpardonedrebels
@DDerrickWest1
Instagram: @dderrickwest1
www.bookbub.com/authors/derrick-west
www.goodreads.com/dderrickwest

For more information about
AMBASSADOR INTERNATIONAL
please connect at:

www.ambassador-international.com
@AmbassadorIntl
www.facebook.com/AmbassadorIntl

If you enjoyed this book, please consider leaving us a review on Amazon, Goodreads, or our website.

More from Ambassador International

We live in an unpredictable, uncontrollable world where things change often, and fear can plant itself deeply within our hearts. *Chickening IN* is a practical approach to defeating the fear and doubt that is preventing us from becoming brave, bold women of God.
Chickening In
by JJ Gutierrez

Nathan and Tammy Whisnant were once overweight, exhausted, and unable to enjoy their grandchildren. But one day, the Holy Spirit convicted them of their need to be the best version of themselves, and together they have now lost nearly a hundred pounds. After working off the weight themselves, the Whisnants decided to share their secret to success with others, and *Imagine Not as Much* was born.
Imagine Not As Much
by Nathan and Tammy Whisnant

Using her own personal journey during an adventurous move to Paris, Anne shares healing truths of Scripture and methods she found to help others find freedom from their baggage. You will be inspired and refreshed as you realize you no longer have to carry your baggage either.
Pack Your Baggage, Honey, We're Moving to Paris!
by Anne Farnum

www.ingramcontent.com/pod-product-compliance
Lightning Source LLC
LaVergne TN
LVHW051518070426
835507LV00023B/3178

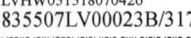